THE FOUND

———

THE LIFE, NATUF
OF ANTHROPO...

THE FOUNDATION STONE

THE LIFE, NATURE AND CULTIVATION OF ANTHROPOSOPHY

RUDOLF STEINER

RUDOLF STEINER PRESS
LONDON

The Foundation Stone translation revised by J Collis
The Life, Nature and Cultivation of Anthroposophy translated
by George Adams and revised by Pauline Wehrle

Rudolf Steiner Press
51 Queen Caroline Street
London W6 9QL

First published as two separate volumes by Rudolf Steiner Press: *The Foundation Stone* (1957, second edition 1979), and *The Life, Nature and Cultivation of Anthroposophy* (1963, reprinted 1976 and 1989)

First edition in a single volume 1996

This book constitutes excerpts from two works originally published in German under the titles *Die Weihnachtstagung zur Begründung der Allgemeinen Anthroposophischen Gesellschaft 1923/24* and *Die Konstitution der Allgemeinen Anthroposophischen Gesellschaft und der Freien Hochschule für Geisteswissenschaft. Der Wiederaufbau des Goetheanum* (volumes 260 and 260a in the *Rudolf Steiner Gesamtausgabe* or Collected Works) by Rudolf Steiner Verlag, Dornach. This authorized translation is published by kind permission of the Rudolf Steiner Nachlassverwaltung, Dornach

A catalogue record for this book is available from the British Library

ISBN 1 85584 075 8

Cover by Andrew Morgan
Typeset by DP Photosetting, Aylesbury, Bucks.
Printed and bound in Great Britain by Cromwell Press Limited, Broughton Gifford, Wiltshire

Contents

PART ONE

THE FOUNDATION STONE

The Laying of the Foundation Stone
of the Anthroposophical Society

Words spoken and written down at Dornach,
Switzerland, 25 December 1923 to 1 January 1924
by Rudolf Steiner

Introduction

by Michael Wilson

This 'Foundation Stone' of the Anthroposophical Society was formed at the Christmas Conference 1923 out of the tragedy a year earlier when the original Goetheanum building had gone up in flames during the last hour of 1922. The foundation stone of that building had been laid into the hill of Dornach during the stormy evening of 20 September 1913. It was a symbol of a deed which was to give visible and tangible form to the creative spirit of the world. The 'stone' consisted of a double pentagon-dodecahedron, made of copper. It was laid in an orientation with the larger of the two forms towards the east where the smaller dome of the building would later stand, and with the smaller form towards the larger dome of the building which would later house the auditorium. To this day it lies buried in its original concrete which now forms part of the foundations of the present building.

Reflection upon the geometrical attributes of the dode-cahedron will show how the original foundation stone lives again in the Foundation Stone verses contained in this book. But the original building itself—half temple, half theatre—could not be repeated. World events made it impossible for it to arise again in any place other than the hearts of human beings. Only there can the human spirit now meet the spirit of the world, and the path along which this may happen is the path of anthroposophy.

It was early in 1913, when a first Anthroposophical Society emerged from the Theosophical Movement, that Rudolf Steiner described how the cosmic wisdom, the heavenly Sophia, had united herself with the evolution of human consciousness—'Philo-Sophia'—and now appeared once more, this time on earth in an objective form: 'Anthropos-Sophia'. This is not a wisdom that can be possessed; but the higher being which slumbers in every one of us can awaken and unite with the Being of Anthroposophia. The verses of this Foundation Stone are a call to us to bring about this awakening, a deed that can take place only within the free human individuality. This new individuality must turn its powers of recognition towards all that the gods have created for it and which makes its life possible, and it must direct its creative will towards the exploration of what awaits it in the spirit. In the balance of the two the individual will find its true humanity.

In working with this meditation we should not forget that when it was originally heard, on Christmas morning 1923, it was the first half of each of the three verses that constituted 'our Foundation Stone', whereas the second halves, which are the Cosmic Reply, came a little later. In this sense the dialogue between the human spirit and the spirit of the world reveals a dramatic depth of meaning.

There are some slight differences in the form in which the verses appear on different pages. This is not a matter of different translations, for Rudolf Steiner himself used slightly different wordings as the Christmas Conference progressed. In the printed version he changed the names of the hierarchical beings into expressions more suited to the wider circle of readers, and when he spoke the words for the first time there were some lines in the second halves of the verses that did not appear in the subsequent versions. We have included these variations as they were originally heard.

The translation of mantric verses poses special problems. Ideally the spiritual experience that every mantra represents should be re-created directly in the language in which it is to be used. To translate a mantric content from one earthly language into another means that the original content can only appear at third hand, and moreover those forms which can be used in one language are sometimes quite impossible in another.

The injunctions to the human soul at the beginning of each verse to practise 'spirit-recalling', 'spirit-awareness' and 'spirit-beholding' need a word of explanation. The first is a translation of *Geist-Erinnern*, which is the activity of going deeply into one's innermost being and recalling the forces that have formed us. It goes beyond what we usually understand by 'memory'. On another occasion Rudolf Steiner spoke of it as 'evolution-memory'. Inasmuch as we can make this into a real experience we shall learn to live our earthly life in a true way. The second injunction is 'practise spirit-awareness' or 'spiritual presence of mind'— *Übe Geist-Besinnen*. It is the awareness of how we stand in living relation to past and future, or to matter and spirit, at every moment of our lives. We can only do this for our-selves. The comfort we receive will be the Grace that comes to us from the Christ Being—the Cosmic Ego. The third injunction to 'practise spirit-beholding'—*Übe Geist-Erschauen*—is the penetration of our spirit into the realm of eternal truth. It is the 'beholding' that takes place when the will is able to transcend human thoughts and come into contact with the world-thoughts themselves. The forming of human knowledge out of pure spiritual experience is a real act of creation.

The threefold nouns that form the last line of the first part of each verse have no corresponding form in English. The first two words are usually adjectival in character while the third is more substantive, but we have to resort to the relatively clumsy construction of 'World-Being of Man' for *Menschen-Welten-Wesen*.

The German verb *walten* so frequently used by Rudolf Steiner has no precise equivalent in English. The nearest is to 'hold sway' or 'prevail' in an impersonal sense. We have followed the example of George Adams in rendering this as 'to wield' but used intransitively as in the alliterative line 'Where in the wielding will of world-creating', which is a picture of the divine creative forces out of which man is born.

The Foundation Conference took place at Christmas, which in German is *Weihnachten*, or '*Weihe-Nacht*', Holy Night. Rudolf Steiner referred to the first Christmas as the *Ur-Weihnacht*, the 'archetypal Christmas'. *Einweihung* is his usual word for initiation. What looks at first sight like a play on words is in reality the perception of truths that lie at a deeper level than our present-day language. In working with a mantra it is often more important to let the sound and the rhythm of the words work on one's imagination rather than to seek a precise definition of their meaning.

Since it is seldom possible to convey the original mantric quality in a single translation, we have included more than one here, in the hope that serious students will work with the one which they find most helpful in leading them towards the original mantric content.

When this content is fully understood it will be seen to be a milestone in human evolution on earth.

Further reading

George Adams' Introduction to the 1957 edition of the present volume, which contains valuable detailed observations on the choice of English equivalents for words in the original German;

F. W. Zeylmans van Emmichoven, *The Foundation Stone* (Rudolf Steiner Press, London 1963);

Rudolf Grosse, *The Christmas Foundation; beginning of a new cosmic age* (Steiner Book Centre, Vancouver 1984);

Rudolf Steiner, *The Christmas Conference for the Foundation of the General Anthroposophical Society 1923/1924* (Anthroposophic Press, New York 1990). This volume contains facsimiles of Rudolf Steiner's notations on the blackboard.

Sergei O. Prokofieff, *Rudolf Steiner and the Founding of the New Mysteries* (Temple Lodge Publishing, London 1994).

The Laying of the Foundation Stone of the Anthroposophical Society

Christmas Day
Tuesday, 25 December 1923

My dear friends,
Let the first words that sound here today be an epitome of what may stand before your souls as the most important findings of recent years.

Later there will be more to say about these words which are, as they stand, a summary. But first let our ears be touched by them, so that out of the signs of the present times and in keeping with our way of thinking, we may renew the ancient Mystery Words: 'Know thyself!'

Soul of Man!
Thou livest in the limbs
Which bear thee through the world of space
Into the spirit's ocean-being.
Practise spirit-recalling
In depths of soul,
Where in the wielding will
Of world-creating
Thine own I
Comes to being
Within God's I.
And thou wilt truly live
In the World-Being of Man.

Soul of Man!
Thou livest in the beat of heart and lung
Which leads thee through the rhythm of time

Into the realm of thine own soul's feeling.
Practise spirit-awareness
In balance of the soul,
Where the surging deeds
Of the world's becoming
Thine own I
Unite
With the World-I.
And thou wilt truly feel
In the Soul-Weaving of Man.

Soul of Man!
Thou livest in the resting head
Which from the grounds of eternity
Opens to thee the world-thoughts.
Practise spirit-beholding
In stillness of thought,
Where the eternal aims of Gods
World-Being's Light
On thine own I
Bestow
For thy free willing.
And thou wilt truly think
In the Spirit-Foundations of Man.

Looking back today on what it has been possible to bring
from the spiritual worlds while the dire storms of war have
been surging through the world, we find it can be epito-
mized in this triad of verses that has just sounded in your
ears. It has been possible to observe the threefold mem-
bering of the human being through which, in the wholeness
of spirit, soul and body, we can reawaken the call 'Know
thyself!' This threefoldness has been perceptible for decades. I myself have only been able to bring it to maturity
over the last ten years, while the storms of war have been
raging.[1] I then tried to indicate how human beings live,

even physically, in their system of metabolism and limbs, in their system of heart and rhythm, and in their system of thinking and perceiving with the head.

When human beings properly take in this threefoldness, bringing their heart to life in the right way through Anthroposophia as indicated yesterday, then, by learning to understand with feeling and with will, they come to know what they are really doing when, enlivened by the World Spirits, they place themselves through their limbs in the widths of space. In taking hold of the world actively (not absorbing it in an inert, passive way, but energetically grasping it in carrying out their duties, their task and mission in the world), human beings discover the being of the all-prevailing human and World Love, which is one member of the whole being of the world.

We may be sure that when human beings learn about the wonderful secret that prevails between lungs and heart—which expresses to inner perception how the world rhythms, working through millennia, throughout the aeons, beat into the pulsing rhythms of the blood and awaken the World Soul in man—when this is wisely comprehended with the heart as organ of cognition, then we may hope that human beings can experience how the God-given World Images manifest the cosmos from within themselves in deeds. As in active movement we grasp the prevailing World Love, so we will grasp the Archetypes of world existence when we feel within ourselves the mysterious transition between world rhythm and heart rhythm, and through this again the human rhythm which takes place mysteriously in a soul-spiritual way between lungs and heart.

When human beings feelingly perceive in the right way what manifests in their head-system, which is at rest there on their shoulders even when they move, then, feeling themselves in their head-system, with the heart's warmth flowing out into their head-system, they will experience within their own being the wielding, working, weaving World Thoughts.

Thus the human being becomes the Trinity of all being: World Love, working in human love; World Imagination, working in the forming of the human organization; and World Thoughts, working mysteriously in the ground of human thoughts. Human beings will comprehend this threefoldness, and will know themselves as free individuals within the prevailing work of the gods in the cosmos; as World Man, individual human being in World Man; working as individual human being within World Man for the world's future. Out of the signs of the present they will renew the ancient words: 'Know thyself!'

The Greeks were still able to leave out the rest, because for them the human self had not yet become so abstract as it is for us, coalesced into the abstract point of the I, or at best into thinking, feeling and will; and because they grasped human nature as a whole in spirit, soul and body. Hence the Greeks were justified in believing that they described the whole human being in spirit, soul and body when they let resound the primal Sun-Words, the Words of Apollo: 'Know thyself!' We, on the other hand, if out of the signs of our time we are to renew these words rightly, must say: 'O Soul of Man, know thyself in the weaving of thy being in spirit, soul and body.' Then we have understood what lies at the very foundation of the whole human being.

In this World Substance there lives and works and has its being the Spirit that streams from the heights and reveals itself in the human head; the Christ-power, working everywhere in the circumference, weaving with the air encircling the earth, works and lives in our breathing system; and the forces in the depths, coming from the interior of the earth, work in our limbs. If at this moment we unite these three, the forces of the heights, the forces of the circumference, the forces of the depths, into one formative

Substance: then in the comprehension of our souls we can confront the dodecahedron of the World with the dodecahedron of Man.

From these three forces—from the Spirit of the heights, from the Christ-power of the circumference, and from the working of the Father, the creative Father-activity that streams upwards from the depths—we *will*, at this moment, to shape in our souls the dodecahedral Foundation Stone, which we lower into the ground of our souls, so that it may there be a steadfast sign in the vigorous foundation of our soul-nature, and so that in the future working of the Anthroposophical Society we may stand on this firm Foundation Stone.

Let us always remain conscious of this Foundation Stone for the Anthroposophical Society which we have shaped today. Let us in future cherish the remembrance of the Foundation Stone planted today in the soil of our hearts, in all that we shall do both here and in the world for the furthering, the evolution, the full unfolding of the Anthroposophical Society. Let us seek in the threefold human being the one who teaches us Love, the one who teaches us World-Imagination, the one who teaches us World-Thoughts. Let us seek in the threefold human being the substance of World-Love which we lay as the foundation; let us seek in the threefold human being the Archetype of Imagination according to which we form the World-Love in our hearts; let us seek the power of Thought from the heights, in order that the dodecahedral Imagination-Picture of Love may ray forth in the appropriate way. Then we shall carry hence what we need; then the Foundation Stone will light up before the eye of our soul, that Foundation Stone which receives from the World-human Love its substance, from the World-human Imagination its living picture-quality, its forming, and from the World-human Thoughts its resplendent light, which whenever we remember this present moment can radiate towards us with light which is warm, and which encourages our action, our thinking, our feeling, and our will.

The right ground in which we must lay today's Foundation Stone, the proper soil, this is our hearts in their harmonious co-operation, in their love-imbued good will to carry the will of anthroposophy through the world together with one another. From the light of Thought, which can at all times ray out to us from the dodecahedral Stone of Love that we today lower into the depths of our hearts, this will radiate towards us like an admonition. We will take this rightly into our souls, my dear friends; with it we will warm our souls, with it we will illumine our souls; and we will guard the warmth of soul and light which with good will we have today planted in our hearts.

We implant it, my dear friends, at a moment when in recollection the one who truly understands the world looks back to that point in human evolution, the turning of the time, when amid the darkness of night and darkness in moral awareness of human beings, striking in as light from heaven, there was born the Divine Being who became the Christ, the Spirit-Being who descended into humankind.

We can best make strong the warmth of soul and light of soul that we need if we quicken them by that warmth and that light which at the turning of the time rayed forth into the darkness of the world as the Light of Christ. Let us now bring this original Christmas—the primal night of initiation which took place two thousand years ago—to life in our own heart, in our mind, in our will, so that this may help us when we want to carry out into the world what radiates towards us through the light of Thought from the dodeca-hedral Foundation Stone of Love, imaging the world and transplanted into the human realm.

So let the feeling of our hearts be turned back to the primal Christmas night in ancient Palestine:

At the turning of the time
The Spirit-Light of the World
Entered the stream of earthly being.
Darkness of night
Had held its sway;
Day-radiant light
Streamed into souls of men.
Light
That gives warmth
To simple shepherds' hearts,
Light
That enlightens
The wise heads of kings.

Light Divine
Christ-Sun!
Warm thou
Our hearts
Enlighten thou
Our heads,

That good may become
What we
From our hearts would found
What we
From our heads would direct
In conscious willing.

This feeling that goes back to the primal Christmas can
give us the strength to warm our hearts and enlighten our
heads, which we need if we are to put into practice in the
right way, working anthroposophically, all that can result
from the knowledge of the human being as a threefold
being harmonizing into one.

Therefore let there now be placed once more like a
summary before our souls what follows from real

comprehension of the words 'Know thyself in spirit, soul and body', let it come before us in the way that it works through the cosmos, so that to our Stone, which we have now laid in the ground of our hearts, there may speak from every direction into our being, into our life, and into our work all that the World has to say to human being, to human life and to human work:

Soul of Man!
Thou livest in the limbs
Which bear thee through the world of space
Into the spirit's ocean-being.
Practise spirit-recalling
In depths of soul,
Where in the wielding will
Of world-creating
Thine own I
Comes to being
Within God's I.
And thou wilt truly live
In the World-Being of Man.

For the Father-Spirit of the heights holds sway
In depths of worlds begetting being:
Seraphim, Cherubim, Thrones!
Let there ring out from the heights
What in the depths is echoed;
And in the echo of the depths
The secret of the heights, resounding
Speaks:
Ex Deo nascimur.

The spirits of the elements hear it
In East, West, North, South:
May human beings hear it.

Soul of Man!
Thou livest in the beat of heart and lung
Which leads thee through the rhythm of time
Into the realm of thine own soul's feeling.
Practise spirit-awareness
In balance of the soul,
Where the surging deeds
Of the world's becoming
Thine own I
Unite
With the World-I.
And thou wilt truly feel
In the Soul-Weaving of Man.

For the Christ-Will in the encircling round holds sway
In the rhythms of worlds, bestowing grace on the soul:
Kyriotetes, Dynamis, Exusiai!
Let there be fired from the East
What in the West is formed;
And the fire of the East,
As it receives form from the West
Speaks:
In Christo morimur.

The spirits of the elements hear it
In East, West, North, South:
May human beings hear it.

Soul of Man!
Thou livest in the resting head
Which from the grounds of eternity
Opens to thee the world-thoughts.
Practise spirit-beholding
In stillness of thought,
Where the eternal aims of Gods
World-Being's Light

On thine own I
Bestow
For thy free willing.
And thou wilt truly think
In the Spirit-Foundations of Man.

For the world-thoughts of the Spirit hold sway
In the being of worlds, craving for light:
Archai, Archangeloi, Angeloi!
Let there be prayed from the depths
What in the heights will be granted.
And when it is rightly understood
How it rings forth from Archai, Archangeloi, Angeloi,
When from the depths is prayed
What in the heights can be answered,
Then speaks it through the world:
Per Spiritum Sanctum reviviscimus.

The spirits of the elements hear it
In East, West, North, South:
May human beings hear it.

Hear it ringing forth in your own hearts, my dear friends!
Then you will found here a true union of human beings for
Anthroposophia, and will carry the Spirit that prevails in
the radiant light of Thought around the dodecahedral Stone
of Love forth into the world, where it will shed light and
warmth for the true progress of human souls, for the progress of the world.

Wednesday, 26 December 1923
... We shall only come to terms among ourselves if at every opportunity we absorb into ourselves what can come as impulses from the spiritual worlds. Therefore ... I should like to bring before you again today at least a part of the words which, at the will of the spiritual worlds, were spoken to you yesterday, so that today, too, we may have them in our souls as an introduction before we proceed to the discussions.

Soul of Man!
Thou livest in the limbs
Which bear thee through the world of space
Into the spirit's ocean-being.
Practise spirit-recalling
In depths of soul,
Where in the wielding will
Of world-creating
Thine own I
Comes to being
Within God's I.
And thou wilt truly live
In the World-Being of Man.

Soul of Man!
Thou livest in the beat of heart and lung
Which leads thee through the rhythm of time
Into the realm of thine own soul's feeling.
Practise spirit-awareness
In balance of the soul,
Where the surging deeds
Of the world's becoming
Thine own I
Unite
With the World-I.
And thou wilt truly feel
In the Soul-Weaving of Man.

Soul of Man!
Thou livest in the resting head
Which from the grounds of eternity
Opens to thee the world-thoughts.
Practise spirit-beholding
In stillness of thought,
Where the eternal aims of Gods
World-Being's Light
On thine own I
Bestow
For thy free willing.
And thou wilt truly think
In the Spirit-Foundations of Man.

We can work rightly with sayings such as these, heard out of the cosmic Word, when we arrange them within our souls in such a way that they cannot leave us. They can become so arranged if you begin by emphasizing those parts that can give you the rhythm. I will first write down for you, my dear friends, one part of what can give you the rhythm:

In the first verse *spirit-recalling*, in the second verse *spirit-awareness*, in the third verse *spirit-beholding*.

Consider this in a rhythmical relationship with what comes about when the human soul is called upon—called upon, that is, by itself—when it is said: 'Thine own I comes to being within God's I'. Consider the corresponding rhythm of 'spirit-awareness' when it is said: 'Thine own I unite with the World-I; and that of 'spirit-beholding' when it is said: 'On thine own I bestow for thy free willing.'

spirit-recalling	*spirit-awareness*	*spirit-beholding*
0	0	0
Thine own I	*Thine own I*	*On thine own I*
Comes to being	*Unite*	*Bestow*
Within God's I	*With the World-I*	*For thy free willing*

In this way, take each single phrase so that it can only stand as it does. Take what sounds as rhythm out of the cosmic rhythm: 'own I in God's I', 'own I in the World-I', 'own I in free willing'; and take the enhancement rising from 'comes to being' to 'unite' to 'bestow', where it passes over into moral sensitivity. Feel the relationship with 'spirit-recalling', 'spirit-awareness' and 'spirit-beholding'. Then in the inner rhythm you will have what during these days the spiritual world is actually bringing to us for the uplifting of our hearts, for the enlightenment of our thinking, for giving wings and enthusiasm to our will.

[The summaries written on the blackboard by Rudolf Steiner are shown in italics.]

Thursday, 27 December 1923
Let us again take into our hearts the words which, out of the
signs of the time, are to give us the necessary self-
knowledge in the right way.

> Soul of Man!
> Thou livest in the limbs
> Which bear thee through the world of space
> Into the spirit's ocean-being.
> Practise spirit-recalling
> In depths of soul,
> Where in the wielding will
> Of world-creating
> Thine own I
> Comes to being
> Within God's I.
> And thou wilt truly live
> In the World-Being of Man.
>
> Soul of Man!
> Thou livest in the beat of heart and lung
> Which leads thee through the rhythm of time
> Into the realm of thine own soul's feeling.
> Practise spirit-awareness
> In balance of the soul,
> Where the surging deeds
> Of the world's becoming
> Thine own I
> Unite
> With the World-I.
> And thou wilt truly feel
> In the Soul-Weaving of Man.
>
> Soul of Man!
> Thou livest in the resting head
> Which from the grounds of eternity

Opens to thee the world-thoughts.
Practise spirit-beholding
In stillness of thought,
Where the eternal aims of Gods
World-Being's Light
On thine own I
Bestow
For thy free willing.
And thou wilt truly think
In the Spirit-Foundations of Man.

Again we will inscribe before our souls a rhythm from these cosmic sayings, in order gradually to penetrate to their structure. We take from the first the words:

Thine own I
Comes to being
Within God's I.

We take from the second verse, which contains within it a second soul process:

Thine own I
Unite
With the World-I.

And from the third verse we take:

On thine own I
Bestow
For thy free willing.

Together with these, in the corresponding rhythm, we write the words which always follow, and which have an inner soul connection with those I have just written down:

And thou wilt truly live
In the World-Being of Man.

And from the second verse:

And thou wilt truly feel
In the Soul-Weaving of Man.

The third verse rounds off the harmony:

And thou wilt truly think
In the Spirit-Foundations of Man.

You will find, my dear friends, that when you pay heed to the inner rhythms that are inherent in these verses, when you then make these inner rhythms present before your soul and bring about in yourself a corresponding meditation, that is, a stillness of thought concerning them, then these utterances are felt as the utterances of world secrets, in so far as these world secrets are resurrected in the human soul as human self-knowledge.

Thine own I
Comes to being
Within God's I
*   live*
World-Being of Man

Thine own I
Unite
With the World-I
*   feel*
Soul-Weaving of Man

On thine own I
Bestow
For thy free willing
*   think*
Spirit-Foundations of Man

Friday, 28 December 1923

Today again I will speak the words which are to give us the foundation for our present work here, and for the further work outside:

Soul of Man!
Thou livest in the limbs
Which bear thee through the world of space
Into the spirit's ocean-being.
Practise spirit-recalling
In depths of soul,
Where in the wielding will
Of world-creating
Thine own I
Comes to being
Within God's I.
And thou wilt truly live
In the World-Being of Man.

For the Father-Spirit of the heights holds sway
In depths of worlds begetting being.

Soul of Man!
Thou livest in the beat of heart and lung
Which leads thee through the rhythm of time
Into the realm of thine own soul's feeling.
Practise spirit-awareness
In balance of the soul,
Where the surging deeds
Of the world's becoming
Thine own I
Unite
With the World-I.
And thou wilt truly feel
In the Soul-Weaving of Man.

For the Christ-Will in the encircling round holds sway
In the rhythms of worlds, bestowing grace on the soul.

Soul of Man!
Thou livest in the resting head
Which from the grounds of eternity
Opens to thee the world-thoughts.
Practise spirit-beholding
In stillness of thought,
Where the eternal aims of Gods
World-Being's Light
On thine own I
Bestow
For thy free willing.
And thou wilt truly think
In the Spirit-Foundations of Man.

For the world-thoughts of the Spirit hold sway
In the being of worlds, craving for light.

We will again, dear friends, inscribe in our souls the inner rhythm that can bring home to us how these very words resound from the cosmic rhythm:

From the first verse:

Practise spirit-recalling

This is the activity that can take place in one's own soul. It corresponds outside in the great World-All with what is expressed in the words:

For the Father-Spirit of the heights holds sway
In depths of worlds begetting being.

The second is:

Practise spirit-awareness

the process within, to which outside in the World-All there answers:

For the Christ-Will in the encircling round holds sway
In the rhythms of worlds, bestowing grace on the soul.

The third is:

Practise spirit-beholding

Outside, there answers:

For the world-thoughts of the Spirit hold sway
In the being of worlds, craving for light.

Practise spirit-recalling
For the Father-Spirit of the heights holds sway
In depths of worlds begetting being.

Practise spirit-awareness
For the Christ-Will in the encircling round holds sway
In the rhythms of worlds, bestowing grace on the soul.

Practise spirit-beholding
For the world-thoughts of the Spirit hold sway
In the being of worlds, craving for light.

Saturday, 29 December 1923
Let us again today hear the words that are to echo in our
soul, both here and when we go out to carry forth what we
here intend:

Soul of Man!
Thou livest in the limbs
Which bear thee through the world of space
Into the spirit's ocean-being.
Practise spirit-recalling
In depths of soul,
Where in the wielding will
Of world-creating
Thine own I
Comes to being
Within God's I.
And thou wilt truly live
In the World-Being of Man.

For the Father-Spirit of the heights holds sway
In depths of worlds begetting being:
Seraphim, Cherubim, Thrones!
Let there ring out from the heights
What in the depths is echoed
Speaking:
Ex Deo nascimur.

Soul of Man!
Thou livest in the beat of heart and lung
Which leads thee through the rhythm of time
Into the realm of thine own soul's feeling.
Practise spirit-awareness
In balance of the soul,
Where the surging deeds
Of the world's becoming
Thine own I

Unite
With the World-I.
And thou wilt truly feel
In the Soul-Weaving of Man.

For the Christ-Will in the encircling round holds sway
In the rhythms of worlds, bestowing grace on the soul:
Kyriotetes, Dynamis, Exusiai!
Let there be fired from the East
What in the West is formed
Speaking:
In Christo morimur.

Soul of Man!
Thou livest in the resting head
Which from the grounds of eternity
Opens to thee the world-thoughts.
Practise spirit-beholding
In stillness of thought,
Where the eternal aims of Gods
World-Being's Light
On thine own I
Bestow
For thy free willing.
And thou wilt truly think
In the Spirit-Foundations of Man.

For the world-thoughts of the Spirit hold sway
In the being of worlds, craving for light:
Archai, Archangeloi, Angeloi!
Let there be prayed from the depths
What in the heights will be granted
Speaking:
Per Spiritum Sanctum reviviscimus.

Let us again take hold of the inner rhythms of these words in meaningful sections. We have here:

Practise spirit-recalling.

What takes place in the human soul relates to all the reality of being within the cosmos of spirit, soul and body. Thus precisely this 'Practise spirit-recalling' points to what then rings forth through the invocation of Seraphim, Cherubim and Thrones, characterizing the manner in which they work in the World-All:

Seraphim, Cherubim, Thrones!
Let there ring out from the heights
What in the depths is echoed.

One actually has the right cosmic image if one pictures in one's soul how from the heights the voices of Seraphim, Cherubim and Thrones ring out within the cosmic Word; and how they are heard, in that they find their echo in the depths of the foundations of world being; and the cosmic Word, evoked from on high, resounding upwards from below, proceeds from Seraphim, Cherubim and Thrones.

In the second verse we have:

Practise spirit-awareness.

This is related to the Second Hierarchy: Kyriotetes, Dynamis, Exusiai. They are characterized if one imagines their voice within the cosmic Word in the sense of the words:

Kyriotetes, Dynamis, Exusiai!
Let there be fired from the East
What in the West is formed.

The third member in human existence is:

Practise spirit-beholding.

This is the indication of the way the Third Hierarchy joins in the cosmic Word:

Archai, Archangeloi, Angeloi!
Let there be prayed from the depths
What in the heights will be granted.

We have here the opposite of the First Hierarchy, where the voices come downwards and echo upwards from below. Here the voices are carried up from the beings who below have a prayer to utter, which from above is then heard. From above downwards: from the heights to the depths; from the circumference: east and west; from below upwards: from the depths to the heights.

Practise spirit-recalling
Seraphim, Cherubim, Thrones
Let there ring out from the heights
What in the depths is echoed.

Practise spirit-awareness
Kyriotetes, Dynamis, Exusiai
Let there be fired from the East
What through the West is formed.

Practise spirit-beholding
Archai, Archangeloi, Angeloi
Let there be prayed from the depths
What in the heights will be granted.

Sunday, 30 December 1923
Let us begin again with the words of human self-knowledge
arising out of the spirit of our time:

Soul of Man!
Thou livest in the limbs
Which bear thee through the world of space
Into the spirit's ocean-being.
Practise spirit-recalling
In depths of soul,
Where in the wielding will
Of world-creating
Thine own I
Comes to being
Within God's I.
And thou wilt truly live
In the World-Being of Man.

Soul of Man!
Thou livest in the beat of heart and lung
Which leads thee through the rhythm of time
Into the realm of thine own soul's feeling.
Practise spirit-awareness
In balance of the soul,
Where the surging deeds
Of the world's becoming
Thine own I
Unite
With the World-I.
And thou wilt truly feel
In the Soul-Weaving of Man.

Soul of Man!
Thou livest in the resting head
Which from the grounds of eternity
Opens to thee the world-thoughts.

Practise spirit-beholding
In stillness of thought,
Where the eternal aims of Gods
World-Being's Light
On thine own I
Bestow
For thy free willing.
And thou wilt truly think
In the Spirit-Foundations of Man.

Today, my dear friends, let us bring together what can speak in a threefold way within the human being:

Practise spirit-recalling,
Practise spirit-awareness,
Practise spirit-beholding.

This can only be rightly united in the human heart by the one who actually appeared at the turning point of time, and in whose Spirit it is our will to work here and strive ever onward:

At the turning of the time
The Spirit-Light of the World
Entered the stream of earthly being.
Darkness of night
Had held its sway;
Day-radiant light
Streamed into souls of men.
Light
That gives warmth
To simple shepherds' hearts,
Light
That enlightens
The wise heads of kings.

Light Divine
Christ-Sun!
Warm thou
Our hearts
Enlighten thou
Our heads,

That good may become
What we
From our hearts would found
What we
From our heads would direct
In conscious willing.

Practise

spirit-recalling   *spirit-awareness*   *spirit-beholding*

That good may become
What we from our hearts would
found
What we from our heads would
direct
In conscious willing.

Monday, 31 December 1923
Again as usual we begin with the saying that we have made
our own:

Soul of Man!
Thou livest in the limbs
Which bear thee through the world of space
Into the spirit's ocean-being.
Practise spirit-recalling
In depths of soul,
Where in the wielding will
Of world-creating
Thine own I
Comes to being
Within God's I.
And thou wilt truly live
In the World-Being of Man.

Soul of Man!
Thou livest in the beat of heart and lung
Which leads thee through the rhythm of time
Into the realm of thine own soul's feeling.
Practise spirit-awareness
In balance of the soul,
Where the surging deeds
Of the world's becoming
Thine own I
Unite
With the World-I.
And thou wilt truly feel
In the Soul-Weaving of Man.

Soul of Man!
Thou livest in the resting head
Which from the grounds of eternity
Opens to thee the world-thoughts.

Practise spirit-beholding
In stillness of thought,
Where the eternal aims of Gods
World-Being's Light
On thine own I
Bestow
For thy free willing.
And thou wilt truly think
In the Spirit-Foundations of Man.

Then we summarize the whole by recalling the event of
Golgotha, which gives to the whole of Earth evolution its
meaning:

At the turning of the time
The Spirit-Light of the World
Entered the stream of earthly being.
Darkness of night
Had held its sway;
Day-radiant light
Streamed into souls of men.
Light
That gives warmth
To simple shepherds' hearts,
Light
That enlightens
The wise heads of kings.

Light Divine
Christ-Sun!
Warm thou
Our hearts
Enlighten thou
Our heads,

That good may become
What we
From our hearts would found
What we
From our heads would direct
In conscious willing.

We take up this

Light Divine
Christ-Sun

in such a way that we relate the final words, which will be spoken again tomorrow in a threefold way, to the manner in which this Light Divine and this Christ-Sun shine out so that they can be heard as radiant suns from East, West, North and South. We relate the final words that were spoken on the first day especially to this Light Divine, this Christ-Sun:

The spirits of the elements hear it
From East, West, North, South:
May human beings hear it.

Light Divine
Christ-Sun

The spirits of the elements hear it
From
East, West, North, South:
May human beings hear it!

Tuesday, 1 January 1924 (morning)
Once more, dear friends, let us take into our souls what
brings us strength during this conference and shall wholly
ensoul us:

> Soul of Man!
> Thou livest in the limbs
> Which bear thee through the world of space
> Into the spirit's ocean-being.
> Practise spirit-recalling
> In depths of soul,
> Where in the wielding will
> Of world-creating
> Thine own I
> Comes to being
> Within God's I.
> And thou wilt truly live
> In the World-Being of Man.
>
> For the Father-Spirit of the heights holds sway
> In depths of worlds begetting being:
> Seraphim, Cherubim, Thrones!
> Let there ring out from the heights
> What in the depths is echoed
> Speaking:
> Ex Deo nascimur.
>
> Soul of Man!
> Thou livest in the beat of heart and lung
> Which leads thee through the rhythm of time
> Into the realm of thine own soul's feeling.
> Practise spirit-awareness
> In balance of the soul,
> Where the surging deeds
> Of the world's becoming
> Thine own I

Unite
With the World-I.
And thou wilt truly feel
In the Soul-Weaving of Man.

For the Christ-Will in the encircling round holds sway
In the rhythms of worlds, bestowing grace on the soul:
Kyriotetes, Dynamis, Exusiai!
Let there be fired from the East
What in the West is formed
Speaking:
In Christo morimur.

Soul of Man!
Thou livest in the resting head
Which from the grounds of eternity
Opens to thee the world-thoughts.
Practise spirit-beholding
In stillness of thought,
Where the eternal aims of Gods
World-Being's Light
On thine own I
Bestow
For thy free willing.
And thou wilt truly think
In the Spirit-Foundations of Man.

For the world-thoughts of the Spirit hold sway
In the being of worlds, craving for light:
Archai, Archangeloi, Angeloi!
Let there be prayed from the depths
What in the heights will be granted
Speaking:
Per Spiritum Sanctum reviviscimus.

We inscribe a simple rhythm into our souls today:

> *Thou livest in the limbs,*
> *For the Father-Spirit of the heights holds sway*
> *In depths of worlds begetting being:*

> *Thou livest in the beat of heart and lung,*
> *For the Christ-Will in the encircling round holds sway*
> *In the rhythms of worlds, bestowing grace on the soul:*

> *Thou livest in the resting head,*
> *For the world-thoughts of the Spirit hold sway*
> *In the being of worlds, craving for light.*

If I write the rhythms in their harmony like this for you, it is because there really does lie within them a replica of the starry constellations. We say: Saturn is in Leo, or Saturn is in Scorpio. On this depend rhythms that fill the world. A primal picture of the spirit lies in such rhythms, as I have written them down for you in the course of these days from our verses, which are inwardly organized throughout in a soul-spiritual way.

The Right Entry into the Spiritual World

The Responsibility We Bear

Tuesday, 1 January 1924 (evening)
As we are together for the last time during this Christmas Conference which should be a source of strength and of vital importance for the Anthroposophical Movement, you will allow me to give this lecture as a supplement to the many vistas opened for us by the series of lectures just finished,[2] while also giving tentative indications concerning the future of anthroposophical endeavour.

When we look at the world today—and it has been the same for years now—destructive elements on a colossal scale are everywhere in evidence. Forces now actively at work foreshadow the abysses into which western civilization will continue to steer. Looking at individuals who are outwardly the cultural leaders in various domains of life, we can perceive that they are in the throes of an ominous, universal sleep. They think, or at least most of them were still thinking only a short while ago, that until the nineteenth century mankind was childish and primitive in respect of understanding and conceptions of the world. Then modern science appeared in its many branches and now—so it is thought—there exists something that must be cultivated as the truth through all eternity.

People who think like this are in fact giving way to extreme arrogance, only they are not aware of it. On the other hand there are also some people today who sense that things are not, after all, as I have just described.

Some little time ago it was still possible for me to give lectures in Germany organized by the Wolff agency.[3] They attracted extraordinarily large audiences so that the existence of a desire for anthroposophy became obvious to many. Among the frequent nonsensical utterances of opponents there was one voice that to be sure was not much cleverer than the others in respect of content, but which nevertheless indicated a remarkable premonition. It consisted in a newspaper report of one of the lectures I had given in Berlin. The report was to this effect: When one listens to something of this kind, one becomes attentive to the fact that something is going on not only on the earth—I am quoting the report approximately—but in the whole cosmos something is happening which summons human beings to adopt a spirituality different from what existed previously. At this time the forces of the cosmos—not only earthly impulses—demand something from human beings; a kind of revolution is taking place in the cosmos, the result of which must be to strive for a new spirituality.

Utterances like this were to be heard, certainly, and were very worthy of note, for the fact of the matter is as follows. The impulse that must be at work in what is now to go out from Dornach will—as I emphasized from every possible point of view during the Conference itself—have to be an impulse originating in the spiritual world, not on the earth. Our endeavour here is to develop the strength to follow impulses from the spiritual world. That is why, in the evening lectures during this Christmas Conference, I have spoken of manifold impulses at work in the course of historical evolution in order that hearts could be opened for the reception of the spiritual impulses which have yet to stream into the earthly world, and which are not derived from that world itself. Everything that has hitherto rightly carried the earthly world has proceeded from the spiritual world. So if we are to achieve anything fruitful for the earthly world, the impulses for such endeavours must be brought from the spiritual world.

This prompts the assertion that the impulses we ought rightly to take with us from this Conference for our further activity must be linked with a great sense of responsibility.

Let us think for a moment of the responsibility laid upon us by this Conference. Anyone with a sense of the reality of the spiritual world has been able to encounter many personalities during recent decades and, observing them spiritually, experience bitter feelings regarding the future destiny of humanity on earth. It has been possible to encounter one's fellow human beings on earth in the way that can be done spiritually and to observe these people during their sleep, while they are in the spiritual world with ego and astral body, having left their physical and ether bodies behind. During recent decades, explorations connected with the destinies of egos and astral bodies while human beings slept have resulted in knowledge calling for great responsibility on the part of those who possess it. One often saw souls, who had left their physical and ether bodies during sleep, approaching the Guardian of the Threshold.

In the course of evolution the Guardian of the Threshold has been brought to human consciousness in very many different ways. Many a legend, many a saga—for it is in this form, not in the form of historical tradition, that things of the greatest importance are preserved—many a legend tells of how, in earlier times, one personality or another met the Guardian of the Threshold and received instruction from him on how to enter the spiritual world and return again to the physical world. Every legitimate entry into the spiritual world must include the possibility of being able at any and every minute to return to the physical world and live here as a practical, thoughtful human being, not as a visionary or an ecstatic mystic.

Fundamentally speaking this has been demanded by the Guardian of the Threshold through all the ages of human endeavours to enter the spiritual world. But notably in the last third of the nineteenth century hardly any human beings who succeeded in approaching the Guardian of the

Threshold in waking consciousness were to be seen. In our present time, when it is historically incumbent upon the whole of mankind to encounter the Guardian of the Threshold in some form, one instead finds souls approaching the Guardian of the Threshold as egos and astral bodies during sleep. These are very significant pictures: the stern Guardian of the Threshold surrounded by groups of human souls in the state of sleep, souls who in waking consciousness lack the strength to approach the Guardian. They approach him while they sleep.

When one watches this scene, a thought arises that is connected with what I have called the seed of great and essential responsibility. The souls approaching the Guardian of the Threshold during the state of sleep plead with the consciousness then prevailing—in the waking state this remains unconscious or subconscious—they plead to be admitted into the spiritual world, to be allowed to cross the threshold. In numberless cases one then hears the voice of the stern Guardian of the Threshold saying: For your own well-being you may not cross the threshold. You may not be allowed to enter the spiritual world. You must go back! For if the Guardian of the Threshold were to permit such souls to enter the spiritual world, they would cross the threshold and enter that world with the concepts imparted to them by the schools, education and civilization of today, with the concepts and ideas with which human beings are obliged to grow up from about the age of six onwards until virtually the end of their lives on earth.

The intrinsic character of these concepts and ideas is such that what human beings become through them in modern civilization and education means that if they enter the spiritual world with them they become paralysed in soul. Moreover, they would return to the physical world empty-headed in respect of thoughts and ideas. If the Guardian of the Threshold were not to reject many human souls of the modern age but allowed them to enter the spiritual world, they would feel on awakening: I am incapable of thinking, my thoughts do not connect with my brain, I am obliged to go through the world void of thoughts. For such is the effect of the abstract ideas that people apply to everything today. They can enter the spiritual world with these ideas but not return from it again with them. When one witnesses this scene which is experienced during sleep by more souls than is usually imagined, one feels: Oh! if only it were possible to protect these souls from having to experience at death what they experience during sleep. For if the condition that is experienced in the presence of the Guardian of the Threshold were to be repeated for a sufficient length of time, if civilization were to remain long enough under the sway of what current education provides, then sleep would become the way of life. Human souls would pass through the gates of death into the spiritual world but would be unable to bring any mental vigour into the next earthly life. It is possible for human beings to enter the spiritual world with the thoughts prevailing today, but they can only return from it again paralysed in soul.

You see, modern civilization can be founded on the form of spiritual life that has for so long been cultivated, but real life does not allow this. Civilization as it now is might continue to progress for a while. During waking life souls would have no inkling of the existence of the Guardian of the Threshold, and during sleep would be rejected by him in order to avoid mental paralysis; and this would finally result in a human race being born in the future with no understanding, no possibility of applying ideas in their future earthly life. All thinking, all ideation would vanish from the earth. A diseased, purely instinctive human race would people the earth. Evil feelings and unbridled emotions without the guiding power of ideas would take hold of the evolution of the souls confronting the Guardian of the Threshold—souls who can gain no entrance to the spiritual world. It is not only this scene that presents the seer with a sorrowful picture, but in a different connection there is another factor as well.

If, on the journey of which I have spoken, when the souls of sleeping human beings confronting the Guardian of the Threshold can be observed, one is accompanied by a human being belonging not to western but to oriental civilization, a terrible reproach for the whole of western civilization may be heard from him, to this effect: If things continue as they now are, then the earth will become barbaric when the human beings living today appear on earth in new incarnations. Human beings will live devoid of ideas, in instincts only. You westerners have brought things to this pass, because you have abandoned the ancient spirituality of the orient.

A glimpse into the spiritual world such as I have described may well bear witness to a strong sense of responsibility as regards the task of human beings. Here in Dornach there must be a place where for those who have ears to hear, direct and significant experiences in the spiritual world can be described. Here there must be a place where sufficient strength is generated not merely to indicate in terms of the dialectic-empirical mentality of today that here or there small traces of spiritual reality exist. If Dornach is to fulfil its task, actual happenings in the spiritual world must be spoken of openly. People must be able to hear of the impulses in the spiritual world which then pour into and control the world of nature. In Dornach people must be able to hear of actual experiences, actual forces, actual beings of the spiritual world. Here there must be the school of true spiritual science. Henceforth we must not shy away from the demands of modern scientific thought which leads human beings in a state of sleep to the stern Guardian of the Threshold. In Dornach the strength must be acquired to confront and experience the spiritual world in its reality.

There must be no dialectical tirades from here on the subject of the inadequacy of modern scientific theory.

Instead I have been obliged to call attention to the position in which human beings are placed when confronting the Guardian of the Threshold on account of these scientific theories and their offshoots in the orthodox schools of today. If what has been said at this Christmas Conference is sincerely applied in the life of soul, the Conference will be a forceful impulse which the soul can then apply in the activity that is needed in this age so that in their next incarnations people may be able to confront the Guardian of the Threshold in the right way, so that civilization itself will meet with the approval of the Guardian of the Threshold.

Compare today's civilization with that of earlier times during all of which people's thoughts and concepts were directed primarily to the supersensible world, to the gods, to the world of productive, generative, creative forces. With concepts that were concerned primarily with the gods, human beings were able to contemplate the earthly world and also to understand it in the light of these concepts and ideas. If with these concepts—worthy of the gods as they were—human beings came before the Guardian of the Threshold, the Guardian would say to them: You may pass, for you bring over the threshold into the supersensible world thoughts that were already directed to the super-sensible world during your earthly life in a physical body. Thus when you return into the physical world of the senses you will have enough strength to protect you from being paralysed by the spectacle of the supersensible world.

Today people develop concepts and ideas which, in accordance with the genius of the age, they want to apply only to the material world. These concepts and ideas are concerned with anything that can be weighed, measured and so on, but they have nothing to do with the gods, and are not worthy of the gods. Hence to souls who have completely succumbed to materialistic ideas that are unworthy of the gods, the voice of the Guardian of the Threshold thunders when they pass before him in a state of sleep: Do not cross the threshold! You have squandered your ideas on the world of the senses. If you do not wish to be paralysed in your life of soul you may not enter the world of the gods as long as you hold such ideas.

These things must be said, not in order to be the subject of argument but because every individual should let his or her mind and soul be permeated by them and thus develop the attitude of mind that should have been generated by this solemn Christmas Conference of the Anthroposophical Society. More important than anything else we take away with us is the recognition of the spiritual world which gives the certainty that in Dornach there will be created a living centre of spiritual knowledge.

Hence a really splendid note was struck this morning when Dr Zeylmans spoke in connection with the realm of medicine, saying that it is no longer possible today for bridges to be built from orthodox science to what it is our aim to found in Dornach. If we were to speak of what it is hoped to develop in the sphere of medicine here by boasting that our research can stand the scrutiny of all modern clinical requirements, then we should never reach any definite goal with regard to our real tasks. For then other people would simply say: That is just a new remedy; and we too have produced plenty of new remedies!

It is of essential importance that a branch of practical life such as medicine should be taken in the real sense into anthroposophical life. That is what I certainly understood to be Dr Zeylmans' wish when he said this morning that an individual who becomes a doctor today really longs for something that gives impulses from a new corner of the world. In the domain of medicine this is precisely what will be done from here in the future, together with many another branch of genuine anthroposophical activity. It will be worked out now, with Dr Wegman as my helper, as a system of medicine based on anthroposophy. This is a dire need of humanity and will soon be available. It is also my intention to establish as soon as possible a close relationship between the Goetheanum and the Clinic in Arlesheim that is proving to be so beneficial. The work there will be oriented entirely towards anthroposophy. That is also Dr Wegman's intention.

In speaking as he did, Dr Zeylmans also indicated what attitude the Executive Council in Dornach will adopt in all spheres of anthroposophical activity. In future we shall know exactly how matters stand. We shall not say: Let us bring eurythmy to this or that town, for if people first see eurythmy without hearing anything about anthroposophy, eurythmy will please them; then, later on perhaps, they will come to us, and because they have liked eurythmy and have heard that anthroposophy is behind it, anthroposophy, too, may please them! Nor shall we say: In the practice of medicine people must be shown that ours are the right remedies, and then they will buy them; later on they may discover that anthroposophy is behind them and then they will come to anthroposophy!

We must have the courage to realize that such a procedure is dishonest and must be abandoned. Anthroposophy will then find its way in the world. Here in Dornach we shall in future strive for truth without fanaticism; we shall work honestly and candidly. Perhaps in this way we can make reparation for principles that have been gravely sinned against in recent years.

We must leave this Conference, which has led to the founding of the General Anthroposophical Society, not with trifling but with solemn thoughts. But I think that nobody will need to carry away any pessimism as a result of what took place here at Christmas. We had, it is true, to walk past the tragic ruins of the Goetheanum every day, but I think that all those who climbed the hill and passed the ruins during the Conference will have become aware of what our friends have understood in their hearts and that the following thought will have become a reality to them:

Spiritual flames of fire will go forth from the new Goetheanum in the future, for the blessing of mankind, out of
our activity and devotion. The greater the courage with
which to conduct the affairs of anthroposophy that we take
with us from the Conference, the more effectively have we
grasped the spiritual impulse of hope that has pervaded the
Conference.

The scene that I have described to you—the scene that is
so often to be observed, of modern human beings with the
results of their civilization and education facing the Guardian of the Threshold in sleep—this scene does not actually
occur among perceptive anthroposophists. But it does
sometimes happen that this warning is necessary: You must
develop the resolute courage to become aware of and avow
your obedience to this voice from the spiritual world, for
you have begun to wake up. Courage will keep you
wakeful; lack of courage—that and that alone could cause
you to sleep.

The voice of exhortation to unfold courage and wake-
fulness—that is the other alternative for anthroposophists
in the life of modern civilization. Non-anthroposophists
hear the voice which says: Remain outside the spiritual
world, for you have misused the ideas that are coined for
purely earthly objects; you have amassed no ideas that are
worthy of the gods. Hence you would be paralysed on your
return into the physical world of the senses. To the souls
who are truly anthroposophical souls, however, it is said:
You have now to be tested in respect only of your courage to
avow adherence to the voice that you can certainly hear and
understand because of the inclination of your souls and
hearts.

My dear friends, a year ago yesterday we were watching
the flames that destroyed the former Goetheanum, but just
as we did not allow ourselves then to be interrupted in our
continuation of the work, so today we are justified in
hoping that when a physical Goetheanum will again be

here, it will be merely the symbol of our spiritual Goetheanum which we will bear with us as an idea when we now go out again into the world.

Over the Foundation Stone laid here will be erected the building in which the single bricks will be the work achieved by individuals in every one of our groups all over the world. We will now turn our thoughts to this work and become conscious of the responsibility of human beings today when they stand before the Guardian of the Threshold who is obliged to forbid them entrance into the spiritual world.

Quite certainly it will never occur to us to feel anything except the deepest pain and sorrow for what happened to us a year ago. But of one thing we may be sure—everything in the world that has achieved some measure of greatness is born from pain. May our own pain be transformed in such a way that a vigorous, light-filled Anthroposophical Society will come into being as the result of your work, my dear friends.

To this end we have pondered deeply the words with which I began this Christmas Conference and with which I want to end it now. May it become for us a festival of consecration not only of a year's beginning but of the beginning of a turning-point of worlds, to which we will dedicate ourselves in selfless cultivation of the spiritual life:

Soul of Man!
Thou livest in the limbs
Which bear thee through the world of space
Into the spirit's ocean-being.
Practise spirit-recalling
In depths of soul,
Where in the wielding will
Of world-creating
Thine own I
Comes to being

Within God's I.
And thou wilt truly live
In the World-Being of Man.

For the Father-Spirit of the heights holds sway
In depths of worlds begetting being:
Seraphim, Cherubim, Thrones!
Let there ring out from the heights
What in the depths is echoed
Speaking:
Ex Deo nascimur.

The spirits of the elements hear it
In East, West, North, South:
May human beings hear it.

Soul of Man!
Thou livest in the beat of heart and lung
Which leads thee through the rhythm of time
Into the realm of thine own soul's feeling.
Practise spirit-awareness
In balance of the soul,
Where the surging deeds
Of the world's becoming
Thine own I
Unite
With the World-I.
And thou wilt truly feel
In the Soul-Weaving of Man.

For the Christ-Will in the encircling round holds sway
In the rhythms of worlds, bestowing grace on the soul:
Kyriotetes, Dynamis, Exusiai!
Let there be fired from the East
What in the West is formed
Speaking:
In Christo morimur.

The spirits of the elements hear it
In East, West, North, South:
May human beings hear it.

Soul of Man!
Thou livest in the resting head
Which from the grounds of eternity
Opens to thee the world-thoughts.
Practise spirit-beholding
In stillness of thought,
Where the eternal aims of Gods
World-Being's Light
On thine own I
Bestow
For thy free willing.
And thou wilt truly think
In the Spirit-Foundations of Man.

For the world-thoughts of the Spirit hold sway
In the being of worlds, craving for light:
Archai, Archangeloi, Angeloi!
Let there be prayed from the depths
What in the heights will be granted
Speaking:
Per Spiritum Sanctum reviviscimus.

The spirits of the elements hear it
In East, West, North, South:
May human beings hear it.

At the turning of the time
The Spirit-Light of the World
Entered the stream of earthly being.
Darkness of night
Had held its sway;
Day-radiant light

Streamed into souls of men.
Light
That gives warmth
To simple shepherds' hearts,
Light
That enlightens
The wise heads of kings.

Light Divine
Christ-Sun!
Warm thou
Our hearts
Enlighten thou
Our heads,

That good may become
What we
From our hearts would found
What we
From our heads would direct
In conscious willing.

My dear friends, carry out into the world your warm hearts in which you have laid the Foundation Stone for the Anthroposophical Society, carry out into the world these warm hearts which promote strong, health-giving activity in the world. Then help will be vouchsafed to you, enlightening your heads in what you would direct in conscious willing. We will set about this today with all possible strength. We shall indeed see, if we prove worthy of this aim, that a good star will hold sway over what is willed from here. Follow this good star, my dear friends! We shall see whither the gods will lead us by the light of this star.

Light Divine
Christ-Sun!
Warm thou

Our hearts
Enlighten thou
Our heads.

The Original Printed Version of the Verses

Rudolf Steiner's explanatory words relating to the text of the Foundation Stone Verses printed for members in the *Nachrichtenblatt* (Members' News Sheet) of 13 January 1924.

In close connection with the opening meeting was the ceremony on the morning of 25 December, which we entitled 'Laying of the Foundation Stone of the Anthroposophical Society'.

It could only be a question of laying a Foundation Stone in an ideal and spiritual sense. The ground in which the Stone was laid was none other than the hearts and souls of those united in the Society, and the Foundation Stone itself must be the mood and spirit springing of its own accord from the anthroposophical way of life. This mood and spirit, so evidently called for by all the signs of the present time, lives in the will to find—by deepening the human soul—the path to an awakened vision of the spirit and to a life proceeding from the spirit. I will now put down the verses in which I tried to give shape to this 'Foundation Stone'.

Menschenseele!
Du lebest in den Gliedern,
Die dich durch die Raumeswelt
In das Geistesmeereswesen tragen:
Übe Geist-Erinnern
In Seelentiefen,
Wo in waltendem
Weltenschöpfer-Sein
Das eigne Ich
Im Gottes-Ich
Erweset;
Und du wirst wahrhaft *leben*
Im Menschen-Welten-Wesen.

Denn es waltet der Vater-Geist der Höhen
In den Weltentiefen Sein-erzeugend.
Ihr Kräfte-Geister
Lasset aus den Höhen erklingen,
Was in den Tiefen das Echo findet;
Dieses spricht:
Aus dem Göttlichen weset die Menschheit.
Das hören die Geister in Ost, West, Nord, Süd:
Menschen mögen es hören.

Menschenseele!
Du lebest in dem Herzens-Lungen-Schlage,
Der dich durch den Zeitenrhythmus
Ins eigne Seelenwesensfühlen leitet:
Übe *Geist-Besinnen*
Im Seelengleichgewichte,
Wo die wogenden
Welten-Werde-Taten
Das eigne Ich
Dem Welten-Ich
Vereinen;
Und du wirst wahrhaft *fühlen*
Im Menschen-Seelen-Wirken.

Denn es waltet der Christus-Wille im Umkreis
In den Weltenrhythmen Seelen-begnadend.
Ihr Lichtes-Geister
Lasset vom Osten befeuern,
Was durch den Westen sich formet;
Dieses spricht:
In dem Christus wird Leben der Tod.
Das hören die Geister in Ost, West, Nord, Süd:
Menschen mögen es hören.

Menschenseele!
Du lebest im ruhenden Haupte,

Das dir aus Ewigkeitsgründen
Die Weltengedanken erschliesset:
Übe *Geist-Erschauen*
In Gedanken-Ruhe,
Wo die ew'gen Götterziele
Welten-Wesens-Licht
Dem eignen Ich
Zu freiem Wollen
Schenken;
Und du wirst wahrhaft *denken*
In Menschen-Geistes-Gründen.

Denn es walten des Geistes Weltgedanken
Im Weltenwesen Licht-erflehend.
Ihr Seelen-Geister
Lasset aus den Tiefen erbitten,
Was in den Höhen erhöret wird;
Dieses spricht:
In des Geistes Weltgedanken erwachet die Seele.
Das hören die Geister in Ost, West, Nord, Süd:
Menschen mögen es hören.

In der Zeiten Wende
Trat das Welten-Geistes-Licht
In den irdischen Wesensstrom;
Nacht-Dunkel
Hatte ausgewaltet;
Taghelles Licht
Erstrahlte in Menschenseelen;
Licht,
Das erwärmet
Die armen Hirtenherzen;
Licht,
Das erleuchtet
Die weisen Königshäupter.

Göttliches Licht,
Christus-Sonne,
Erwärme
Unsere Herzen;
Erleuchte
Unsere Häupter;

Dass gut werde,
Was wir
Aus Herzen gründen,
Was wir
Aus Häuptern
Zielvoll führen,
Wollen.

Alternative Translation of the Printed Version

by George Adams (1927)

Soul of Man!
Thou livest in the limbs
Which bear thee through the world of Space
Into the ocean-being of the Spirit.
Practise *Spirit-recollection*
In depths of soul,
Where in the strength sublime
Of world-creative life
Thine own I grows to full being
In the I of God.
Then in the being of the World of Man
Thy *Life* will be true.

For the Father-Spirit of the Heights
Reigns in the depths of the World, begetting life.
Spirits of Strength!
May there ring forth from the Heights
The call that is re-echoed in the Depths,
Saying:
From the Divine springeth Mankind.
Spirit-beings hear it in East and West and North and
    South:
May human beings hear it!

Soul of Man!
Thou livest in the beat of heart and lung
Which guides thee through the rhythm of the Ages
Into the feeling of thine own Soul-being.
Practise *Spirit-meditation*

In the balance of the soul,
Where the surging deeds
Of cosmic evolution
Unite thine own I
With the I of the World.
Then in the working of the Soul of Man
Thy *Feeling* will be true.

For the Christ-Will in this horizon's Round
Reigns in the rhythms of the World, blessing the soul.
Spirits of Light!
May there be kindled from the East
The flame that is moulded by the West,
Saying:
In Christ Death becomes Life.
Spirit-beings hear it in East and West and North and
    South:
May human beings hear it!

Soul of Man!
Thou livest in the resting head
Which from the wellsprings of Eternity
Unlocks for thee the Thoughts of the World.
Practise *Spirit-penetration*
In restfulness of thought,
Where the eternal aims of God
Grant light of cosmic being
To thine own I
For free and active Will.
Then in the spiritual founts of Man
Thy *Thought* will be true.

For the Cosmic Thoughts of the Spirit
Reign in the being of the World, praying for light.
Spirits of Soul!
May there ascend from the Depths

The prayer that is heard in the Heights,
Saying:
In the cosmic Spirit-Thoughts the Soul awakes.
Spirit-beings hear it in East and West and North and
    South:
May human beings hear it!

At the turning-point of time,
The Spirit-Light of the World
Entered the stream of Earthly Evolution.
Darkness of Night
Had held its sway;
Day-radiant Light
Poured into the souls of men:
Light that gave warmth
To simple shepherds' hearts,
Light that enlightened
The wise heads of kings.

O Light Divine!
O Sun of Christ!
Warm Thou our hearts,
Enlighten Thou our heads,
That good may become
What from our hearts we would found
And from our heads direct
With single purpose.

Alternative Translation of the Printed Version

by Pauline Wehrle

Human Soul!
You live in the limbs
Which bear you through the world of space
Within the flowing ocean of the spirit:
Practise *spirit re-cognition*
In depths of soul,
Where in the wielding will
Of world creating
The individual I
Comes to being
In the I of God;
And you will truly *live*
In your body's cosmic being.

For the Father Spirit of the heights is present
In world depths begetting existence:
Spirits of Strength!
May there ring forth from the heights
The call re-echoed in the depths;
Proclaiming:
Humankind is born of God.
The elemental spirits hear it
In east, west, north, south:
*May hu*man beings *hear it!*

Human Soul!
You live in the beat of heart and lung
Which leads you through the rhythm of time
Into the realm of your own soul's feeling.

Practise *spirit presence*
In soul composure,
Where the weaving deeds
Of universal becoming
Unite
The individual I
With the I of the World;
And you will truly *feel*
In the active life of your soul.

For the Christ Will is present all around
In world rhythms shedding grace on our souls;
Spirits of Light!
May what is formed by the west
Have been quickened in the light of the east;
Proclaiming:
In Christ death becomes life.
The elemental spirits hear it
In east, west, north, south:
*May hu*man beings *hear it!*

Human Soul!
You live in the stillness of the head
Which from the founts of eternity
Discloses for you cosmic thoughts:
Practise *spirit beholding*
In thought calm,
Where the eternal aims of Gods
Give the light of spirit worlds
To the individual I
For will in freedom.
And you will truly *think*
In the founts of your human spirit.

For the Spirit's cosmic thoughts are present
In world existence begging for light;

Spirits of Soul!
May there ascend from the depths
The plea heard in the heights;
Proclaiming:
In the Spirit's cosmic thoughts the soul will awaken.
The elemental spirits hear it
In east, west, north, south:
*May hu*man beings *hear it!*

At the turning of time
Cosmic Spirit Light descended
Into the earthly stream of being;
Darkness of night
Had run its course;
The light of day
Shone forth in human souls:
Light
That gives warmth
To poor shepherds' hearts,
Light
That enlightens
The wise heads of kings.

God-given light,
Christ Sun
Give warmth
To our hearts;
Give light
To our heads;
That what we found
From our hearts
What we guide
From our heads
Will be good.

Alternative Translation of the Printed Version

by Richard Seddon

Soul of Man!
You live within the limbs
Which bear you through the world of Space
Into the ocean-being of the spirit:
Practise *spirit-remembering*
In depths of soul,
Where in the sovereign
World-Creator presence
One's own I
Within God's I
Gains Being;
And you shall truly *live*
In cosmic Being of Man.

For the Father Spirit of the heights holds sway
In the depths of worlds begetting existence:
Spirits of Power
Let from the heights ring out
What in the depths is echoed;
This resounds:
From the Divine mankind has Being.
    This the spirits hear in East, West, North South;
    May men hear it.

Soul of Man!
You live within the beat of heart and lung
Which leads you through the rhythms of Time
Into your own soul-nature's weaving feelings:
Practise *spirit-awareness*

In balance of the soul,
Where the on-surging
Deeds of world-becoming
One's own I
And I of world
Unite;
And you shall truly *feel*
In the soul-working of Man.

For the Will of Christ all around holds sway
In the world rhythms bestowing grace on souls:
Spirits of Light!
Let from the East flame up
What through the West takes form;
This resounds:
In Christ death becomes life.*
        This the spirits hear in East, West, North, South;
        May men hear it.

Soul of Man!
You live within the resting head
Which from the grounds of eternity
Reveals the universal thoughts:
Practise *spirit-beholding*
In the calm of thought,
Where the eternal aims of Gods
World-Being's light
On one's own I
Bestow
For will in freedom;
And you shall truly *think*
In spirit foundations of Man.

---

* May also be read: In Christ life becomes death. (In Christo morimur—In
Christ we die.)

For the spirit's cosmic thoughts hold sway
In world Being beseeching light:
Spirits of Soul!
Let from the depths be entreated
What in the heights finds hearing;
This resounds:
In the Spirits cosmic thoughts the soul awakes.
    This the spirits hear in East, West, North, South;
    May men hear it.

At the turning of the times
Cosmic Spirit Light descended
Into the earthly stream of Being:
Darkness of night
Had run its course;
Day-bright light
Shone forth in human souls;
Light
That brings warmth
To simple shepherds' hearts;
Light
That illumines
The wise heads of kings.

Godly Light,
Christ Sun,
Set aglow
Our hearts,
Illuminate
Our heads,
That good may be
What we
From hearts would found,
What we
From heads would guide,
In steadfast will.

Notes and References to Part One

1 For the first time in the public lecture in Berlin on 15 March 1917 in R. Steiner, *Geist und Stoff, Leben und Tod* (GA 66) (Dornach, 1988), and *The Case for Anthroposophy* (GA 21), tr. O. Barfield (London, Rudolf Steiner Press, 1977).

2 R. Steiner, *World History in the Light of Anthroposophy* (GA 233), tr. G. & M. Adams (London, Rudolf Steiner Press, 1977).

3 In 1921 and 1922, the largest German concert agency of the day, Wolff & Sachs in Berlin, had organized a number of lecture tours for Rudolf Steiner.

PART TWO

THE LIFE, NATURE AND CULTIVATION OF ANTHROPOSOPHY

*Letters to Members of the
Anthroposophical Society*

Introductory Note

After the Foundation Meeting of the General Anthroposophical Society in Dornach (Christmas, 1923–24), Rudolf Steiner wrote week by week '*Articles*' addressed to the members, as well as a number of independent 'Leading Thoughts'. They were published in the members' supplement to the Goetheanum weekly, and in the English edition of it, *Anthroposophical Movement*. From the autumn of 1924 Steiner wrote '*Letters*' to members with 'Leading Thoughts' as summaries (published in book form in 1926 as *The Michael Mystery*, now available, together with the earlier independent Leading Thoughts, under the title *Anthroposophical Leading Thoughts—The Michael Mystery*).

The present volume contains the earlier '*Articles*,' which describe the character of the Society arising from the Foundation Meeting and give advice as to its conduct and relation to the world.

Further reading

By Rudolf Steiner

Anthroposophical Leading Thoughts: Anthroposophy as a Path of Knowledge: The Michael Mystery (Rudolf Steiner Press, 1973).

World History in the Light of Anthroposophy. Eight lectures given during the Christmas Foundation Meeting (Rudolf Steiner Press, 1950).

Karmic Relationships: Esoteric Studies. Volumes I to VIII (Rudolf Steiner Press).

Letters to the Members

*The Founding of the General Anthroposophical Society at the
Christmas Conference, 1923, Dornach, Switzerland*

The purpose of the Christmas Conference[1] which has just
finished was to give the Anthroposophical Society the form
most suitable for the cultivation of the anthroposophical
movement. A society of this kind cannot have abstract rules
or statutes, for its foundation is already there in the insights
into the spiritual world which are presented as anthroposophy. By now a large number of men and women have
already found in anthroposophy an impulse which satisfies
their spiritual endeavours. The union in a society with
others of a like mind is what their souls require, for in
mutual give and take in spiritual matters human life
unfolds its truest essence. Therefore it follows that those
who want to make anthroposophy an integral part of their
lives would like to have a society through which to foster it.

Anthroposophy has its roots in the perceptions—already
gained—into the spiritual world. Yet these are only the
roots. The branches, leaves, blossoms and fruits of anthroposophy grow and spread out into all the fields of human
life and action. With thoughts which manifest the essence
and laws of spiritual being the call of anthroposophy rings
into the very depths of the creative human soul, where
artistic powers are conjured forth. Art receives incentives
on all sides. Anthroposophy pours into human hearts the
warmth which is kindled when the eyes of the soul are
lifted to the spiritual world. In genuine devotion to the
Divine Presence in the world the religious sense is awakened, and religion itself is much deepened and intensified.

The wellsprings of anthroposophy are opened for the

human will—strengthened by love—to draw from them. Kindling the love of humankind, anthroposophy grows creative in moral impulses to action and in the practice of a truly social life.

Anthroposophy fructifies with the fertile seeds of spirit vision our observation of nature, thus changing learnedness into a true knowledge of nature.

In all these ways anthroposophy generates a multitude of vital tasks, but these can only find their way into the wider circles of human life if they are first of all fostered in a society.

The responsible people at the Goetheanum in Dornach issued an invitation—a call to those who are convinced that anthroposophy, in the way it is cultivated there, is seeking to be equal to these tasks. These were invited to a Christmas Conference where the efforts which had been going on for some time past in the founding of various anthroposophical societies should be brought to an adequate culmination.

The response was beyond expectation. Seven to eight hundred people came to the 'Laying of the Foundation Stone' of the 'General Anthroposophical Society'.[2] The proceedings shall be described by gradual instalments in the 'Goetheanum' supplement. It fell to me to open and conduct the meetings. It was with a glad heart that I did the opening. Beside me sat the Swiss poet Albert Steffen. The whole gathering of anthroposophists looked towards him with thankful hearts. It was on Swiss soil that they had come together to found the Anthroposophical Society. In Albert Steffen they have long been indebted to Switzerland for a leading member to whom they look up with genuine enthusiasm. In him I had Switzerland before me represented by one of the noblest of its sons; and my first words were of heartfelt greetings to him and all our friends in Switzerland. My second words were to call on him to give the opening address.

It was a deeply moving one. Here spoke Albert Steffen,

the wonderful painter in words, the sculptor of poetic images. Soul-stirring images arose before us as visions as we listened to him. There appeared before our mind's eye the moment when we laid the Foundation Stone of the Goetheanum in 1913. I cannot find words to describe what I experienced when the ceremony in which I had been privileged to take part ten years since arose before me once again in Steffen's picture.

Words shaped to artistic perfection conjured up in our minds the building of the Goetheanum—hundreds of devoted hands at work, hundreds of hearts beating with united enthusiasm.

Then—the burning of the Goetheanum.[3] The whole tragedy of it, the pain of many thousands throbbed again as Albert Steffen spoke.

And then another picture: in the foreground the very Being of Anthroposophy transfigured in the soul of the poet; and in the background the enemies—not blamed but simply portrayed with all his formative power of expression.

'Ten years of Goetheanum'—one could feel how deeply Albert Steffen's words sank into the hearts of those present.[4]

After this prelude, so worthy of the occasion, it fell to me to speak about the form which the Anthroposophical Society should now assume.

I had to say what should take the place of ordinary statutes. What had to come in their place was a *description* of what it is that human beings desire to achieve in that they come together on a purely human basis as the Anthroposophical Society. It is at the Goetheanum, in the makeshift wooden huts we have had since the fire, that anthroposophy is being fostered. I had to say how the leaders at the Goetheanum envisaged this task, and what they considered its effect would be on human civilization. Then a description had to follow of their conception of the administration of a 'School of Spiritual Science'. It was not a matter of setting up principles to be acknowledged but of *characterizing* a reality. To this we simply add: Anyone wanting to participate in what is being done at the Goetheanum can become a member.

Here are the only proposals we make in the way of statutes—although these are no 'statutes' but a description of what can result from the kind of purely human and living social relationship indicated above:

1. The General Anthroposophical Society is meant to be a union of people who desire to further the life of the soul, both in the individual and in human society, on the basis of a true knowledge of the spiritual world.

2. The persons gathered at the Goetheanum, Dornach, at Christmas 1923—both the individuals who were present and the groups which were represented—form the foundation of this Society. They are convinced that there is in existence at the present time a real science of the spiritual world—elaborated for years past and, in important particulars, already published, and that today's civilization lacks the cultivation of such a science. This is to be the task of the General Anthroposophical Society. It will endeavour to fulfil the task by making the spiritual science of anthroposophy fostered in the Goetheanum at Dornach the central point of its activities, with all that results from it, for brotherhood in social life, for the moral and religious life of humanity, as well as for the life of art and human cultural life altogether.*

3. The persons gathered together at Dornach in founding the Society recognize and support in the following particulars the view of those responsible at the Goetheanum and now represented by the Executive Council formed at the Foundation Conference:

---

* The Society is a continuation of the Anthroposophical Society founded in 1912. With the same objects in view which were then defined, the intention is to create an independent point of departure, in keeping with the true spirit of the time.

'Anthroposophy, as pursued in the Goetheanum, leads to results which can be of assistance to every human being— without distinction of nationality, social standing or religion—as an incentive in spiritual life. These results can in a real sense give rise to a social life based on brotherly love. The possibility of making them one's own and founding life upon them depends on no special degree of learning or education, but alone on free, unbiased human nature. The researches, however, which lead to them and to the power of competent judgement on the result of research, are subject to a spiritual-scientific training which has to be acquired step by step. These results are in their way as exact as those of natural science. When they attain general recognition like these, they will bring about similar progress in all spheres of life, not only in the spiritual but also in the practical domain.'

4. The Anthroposophical Society is in no sense a secret society, but an entirely public one. Without distinction of nationality, social standing, religion, scientific or artistic conviction, any person who considers the existence of such an institution as the Goetheanum in Dornach in its capacity as School of Spiritual Science to be justified, can become a member of the Society. The Anthroposophical Society is averse to any kind of sectarian tendency. Politics it does not consider to be among its tasks.

5. The Anthroposophical Society looks upon the School of Spiritual Science at Dornach as the centre of its work. This will be composed of three classes. Members of the Society will—on application—be admitted to the School after a period of membership to be determined by those responsible at the Goetheanum. They thus gain entrance to the first class of the School of Spiritual Science. Applicants will be received into the second or third class respectively when those responsible at the Goetheanum consider them fit.

6. Every member of the Anthroposophical Society has the right to participate—under conditions to be announced by the Executive Council—in all lectures, performances and meetings of any kind arranged by the Society.

7. The establishment of the School of Spiritual Science devolves in the first place on Rudolf Steiner, who will appoint his collaborators and his possible successor.

8. All publications of the Society will be open to the public as are those of other public societies.* The same will apply to the publications of the School of Spiritual Science; but in regard to *these* works those responsible for the School reserve the right from the outset to deny the validity of opinions unsupported by qualifications, namely by the training from which these works proceed. In this sense, and as is customary in the recognized scientific world, they will admit the validity of no judgement which is not based on the requisite preliminary studies. The publications of the School of Spiritual Science will therefore contain the following notice: 'Printed in manuscript for the members of the School of Spiritual Science, Goetheanum, class ... No person is held qualified to form a judgement on the contents of these works who has not acquired—through the School itself or in an equivalent manner recognized by the School—the requisite preliminary knowledge. Other opinions will be in so far disregarded as the authors of the works in question are not willing to take them on as a basis for discussion.'

9. The object of the Anthroposophical Society will be the furtherance of research in the spiritual realm; that of the School of Spiritual Science the actual pursuit of such research. A dogmatic approach in any sphere whatsoever does not belong in the Anthroposophical Society.

10. The Anthroposophical Society holds an annual general meeting in the Goetheanum once a year, when the Executive Council submits a full report and balance sheet.

---

* The conditions of entry to the School have up to now been made public and will continue to be so.

The agenda shall be issued by the Executive Council together with the invitation to all members six weeks before the meeting. The Executive Council may summon extraordinary general meetings and fix the agenda for such meetings. Invitations to such meetings shall be sent to members three weeks in advance. Motions by individual members or groups of members shall be sent in a week before the meeting.[5]

11. The members may join together in smaller or larger groups on any geographical or relevant basis of activity. The seat of the Anthroposophical Society is at the Goetheanum, whence the Executive Council shall communicate to the members or groups of members what it considers to be the task of the Society. It enters into communication with the officials elected or appointed by the various groups. The individual groups attend to the admission of members; however, the applications should be presented to the Executive Council in Dornach, where they are signed in trust for the group officials. As a general rule every member should join a group. Only those for whom it is quite impossible to find admission to a group should apply directly to Dornach to become a member.

12. The subscription shall be fixed by the individual groups; each group shall however send 15 Swiss francs annually per member to the headquarters of the Society at the Goetheanum.

13. Each working group formulates its own statutes, but these must not be incompatible with the statutes of the Anthroposophical Society.

14. The organ of the Society is the weekly *Das Goetheanum* which shall for this purpose issue a supplement containing the official communications of the Society. This enlarged edition of *Das Goetheanum* will be supplied to members of the Anthroposophical Society only.

Intimately connected with the opening meeting on the morning of December 25 was the festivity, also on the morning of December 25, entitled 'The Laying of the Foundation Stone of the General Anthroposophical Society'. It could only be a question of laying a foundation stone in an ideal and spiritual sense. The soil in which the stone was laid could be no other than the hearts and souls of those united in the Society. And the Foundation Stone itself must be the attitude of mind which arises when anthroposophy shapes one's life. This attitude to life, formed in the way required by the signs of the present times, lies in the will to find—through the deepening of the human soul—the path to an awakened vision of the spirit and to a life proceeding from the spirit. I will give the further description of the opening gathering in the next number of the *News Sheet*.

The Executive Council
of the General Anthroposophical Society

The Executive Council was formed at the Christmas Conference of persons who through the nature of their connection with the life of anthroposophy will be able, from the Goetheanum, to take the initiative for action in the manner indicated in these paragraphs. They must be persons whose work is situated at the Goetheanum itself. How they relate to the other functionaries of the Society will be discussed in future numbers of the *News Sheet*. At present only their names will be given:

President: Dr Rudolf Steiner
Vice-President: Albert Steffen
Recording Secretary: Dr Ita Wegman
Committee Members: Frau Marie Steiner
Fräulein Lili Vreede
Secretary and Treasurer: Dr Günther Wachsmuth

This Executive Council will be called the Founding Executive Council in Paragraph 15 of the statutes.

The next *News Sheet* will contain:

1. Rudolf Steiner—an appeal to the members.
2. Continuation of the report on the Christmas Conference.
3. Constitution of the Society.
4. The School of Spiritual Science.

It would be desirable that the *News Sheet* be published in translation for the members in other countries. We ask the general secretaries or councils of the various societies and groups to make proposals to us on the subject of these translations.

To the Members—I

20 January 1924

The full content of the Christmas Conference for the Founding of the General Anthroposophical Society was certainly not yet grasped in what the members experienced while they were gathered together at the Goetheanum. Only if, in the future, all those everywhere who love anthroposophy begin to feel that it is through the very fact of their putting into effect the inspirations coming from that conference that new anthroposophical life is coming into being, only then will its content really have been grasped. If this were not so the conference would not have fulfilled its task. Such were doubtless the feelings of all those who took part in it.

We have fostered the life of anthroposophy for more than 20 years. Members who have worked together for it in the forms of association which we had till now need only let their own experience speak and they will understand why the effort was made from the Goetheanum to bring a new impulse.

Anthroposophical endeavour grew out of small beginnings. A few people within the framework of the Theosophical Society came together to share in what was then presented in the special form of anthroposophy. All they wanted, to begin with, was to learn of anthroposophy and enable it to become fruitful in their lives. It was in little circles and unambitious public gatherings we spoke about the spiritual world, the nature of the human being and the way knowledge of these things is attained. Scarcely anyone outside the circle of those who attended the meetings concerned themselves with what was being presented there. Many of those who did take part found what they had been seeking in the deepest longings of their hearts. These either became faithful and quiet adherents or more or less enthusiastic fellow workers. Others did not find it and, on noticing this, stayed away. It all proceeded quietly and without disturbance from outside.

It remained like this for many years. We worked on the fundamental elements of insight into soul and spirit. Indeed we were able to go very far in this. Opportunities could be created for those who had been engaged in anthroposophy for a long time to rise from basic to higher truths. The foundations of anthroposophy were laid not only as a spiritual scientific system of knowledge but as a living impulse in many human hearts.

But anthroposophy goes to the very roots of human existence, and there it comes together with all that grows out of human life and work. Therefore it was natural for its activities to spread by-and-by to a wide variety of spheres of human life and work.

A beginning was made in art. In the mystery plays artistic shape was given to what spiritual sight revealed about the world and humankind. To many members it was a source of deep satisfaction to receive again in artistic presentation what they had hitherto absorbed, without external pictures, in their hearts and minds.

Here again, no one outside the circle of those directly involved paid much attention.

Then it came about that keen and devoted anthroposophists conceived the plan of building a home of its own for the movement. In 1913 we laid the foundation stone of what later on was called the Goetheanum, and it was built in the years that followed.

Something else took place at this time. Men and women whose life-work lay in one or another branch of science or academic learning had gradually come into the Society. For these people, too, the original motive for joining was certainly the same common human need of the heart and soul. They wanted to find, in their own souls, the paths which lead to the light of the spirit. But their scientific training and experience had also shown them that the prevailing scientific views invariably fail at the very point where it becomes a burning need of human beings to have conclusive knowledge. Here the accepted ideas come to a dead end. Our friends perceived that the various sciences—if fertilized by anthroposophy—might be taken further where, with the methods adopted hitherto, they filter into nothingness. Thus anthroposophical work arose in many spheres of science and scholarship.

Because of the Goetheanum and because of this scientific work the Anthroposophical Society now came before the public eye, and the peaceful and undisturbed activity it had hitherto enjoyed came to an end. The world became aware of anthroposophy; people outside its own circles began to ask whether it had anything worthwhile to offer. Inevitably some turned out to hold convictions that differed from what anthroposophy had found, or who had been attached to something which anthroposophy revealed in a light which did not please them. They began to pass judgement on anthroposophy from their own points of view.

For the results which rapidly ensued the Anthroposophical Society was altogether unprepared. It had been a centre of peaceful work; and in such work by far the greater number of members had found complete satisfaction. They believed nothing more was expected of them beyond the duties which were theirs through their place in outer life.

And who can say they were not fully justified in so thinking? When human beings turn away dissatisfied from other things and come to anthroposophy they naturally want to find in it the positive side of spiritual knowledge and spiritual life. They feel disturbed in their search if they encounter on all sides attacks on anthroposophy.

A solemn question has indeed arisen for the Anthroposophical Society. How can the true pursuit of spiritual life be continued in the way that spiritual life requires, although the time is past when anthroposophy was left alone except by those who take a positive part in it? Those responsible at the Goetheanum saw one of the pertinent questions in this light: Ought we not to realize that the Anthroposophical Society must work to embody even *more* anthroposophy than hitherto? And how can this be done?

Beginning from these questions, I will continue my address to members in the next number of the *News Sheet*.

To the Members—II

27 January 1924

The Right Relationship of the Society to Anthroposophy

Anthroposophy is there for human beings who are seeking in their souls the path to a conscious experience of the spirit.

To fulfil its purpose the Anthroposophical Society must be in a position to serve those who are seeking. It must itself, as a society, find its true relationship to anthroposophy.

Anthroposophy can only thrive as a living thing. Its fundamental character is life, life flowing from the spirit. Hence it needs to be fostered by the living soul, in warmth of heart.

The basic form in which anthroposophy can appear among human beings is that of idea; the first door at which it knocks is that of insight. If this were not so it would have no substance but would be a mere feeling of rapture. The true spirit does not 'go into raptures', it speaks a language that is precise and full of content.

But this language speaks to the whole human being and not only to the intellect. A person who wanted to receive anthroposophy only with the intellect would kill it in the very act. He may well come to the conclusion that it is 'cold and scientific'. He does not see that it first lost its warm life by the kind of reception he gave it in his soul.

Anthroposophy, to have existence in our time, must use the means which the civilization of today provides. It must find its way to people in books and lectures. Yet in its nature it is not of the library shelf. It must be born anew in the human heart whenever a person opens a book to learn from it. This can only be the case if the author looked into the hearts of his fellow human beings while he was writing it in order to discover what he must say to them. However, an author can only do this if he is touched by the living spirit as he writes. Then he will confide to the dead written word something which the soul of the reader can feel to be a resurrection of the spirit from the word. Books that can come to life in the human being as he reads—these alone may be called anthroposophical.

Still less than the dead book can anthroposophy abide the speaking book, where human speech wears the dead mask of life. It often happens in our civilization that we feel no difference between the reading of a book or article and listening to a human being. When we listen to some speakers, we make acquaintance not with a human being but with the thoughts he has been thinking. We feel that he might just as well have written them.

Anthroposophy does not tolerate being taken up only in this way. When we hear anthroposophy from a fellow human being we want to experience his own unique being. We do not want a spoken essay.

Therefore, while it *must* also live in written works, anthroposophy can be born anew in every gathering of human beings where through the spoken word it seeks admission to human souls. But this will only happen if the speaking is between one human being and another and not the mere thoughts they have absorbed.

Anthroposophy—for this very reason—cannot find its way through the world by ordinary agitation or propaganda, no matter how well meant. Agitation kills real anthroposophy. Anthroposophy must come forward because the spirit compels it to do so. It must confirm its life because life cannot but manifest itself. But it may never force its existence on people. Waiting always for those to come who want it, it must be far removed from all coercion—even the coercion of persuasion.

This is the frame of mind which I want to bring home to members as something that is most needed. This indeed should grow out of our Christmas Conference. We have often met with resistance simply because in our hearts we did not always remain true to this frame of mind. Often, though we strove to have it, we failed to maintain it in the way we expressed ourselves. Our very words must reflect not the propagandist's attempt to persuade but the desire to give expression to the spirit.

If we hold anthroposophy in our hearts in this way then it will become something *larger* than what has often lived in our groups in the past. The Goetheanum has the will to do all its work in this spirit, the spirit that was actually made visibly manifest in the artistic forms of the building we have lost. While the building was still there, then if the spoken word went astray and introduced a note of attack it immediately called forth from the very forms of the building a shrill dissonance. The Goetheanum, when rebuilt, will only be a thing of truth if the Anthroposophical Society everywhere has the will to be a living witness to its truth. We must not think—least of all in anthroposophy—that we can only be effective if we force things. Something that lives out of the strength of its own intrinsic spirit can wait until the world is ready to receive what it has to give.

When this frame of mind is alive in every group of the Anthroposophical Society then the spirit of anthroposophy will be able to send its influence beyond our circles, where it is our task to put anthroposophy before the world. We must not surround ourselves with an artificial air of mystery. The time in which we live will not suffer pretence. Everything must come out into the open. The real 'secret' will not depend on secretiveness but on the inner earnestness with which anthroposophy has to be experienced anew in every human heart. It cannot be transmitted by external means. It is only by inner experience that each soul can grasp it. Thus it becomes a 'secret' which must be unsealed each time anew in our understanding. When we grasp *this* kind of 'secret' we shall have the right 'esoteric' attitude in our souls.

To the Members—III

3 February 1924

Members' Meetings

It happened not infrequently that people became members of the Anthroposophical Society for the sole reason that they could then buy books which were not sold outside. Such members took little interest in the life of the groups in the Society. Having perhaps attended the meetings to start with, they soon stayed away, saying, 'What goes on in these groups is of no help to me. I shall get hold of anthroposophy better by working at it alone.'

It cannot be denied that the reproaches made in this way against the members' meetings were not always reasonable. The trouble did not always lie in the meetings, but often in the impossible demands of those people who could not find their right relation to them.

It is easy to say, 'This or that does not satisfy me.' It is more difficult quietly to observe what is unsatisfactory, and then *oneself* to make the necessary efforts to help things improve. On the other hand there is no reason to conceal the fact that in the members' meetings some things call for change.

It is precisely in meetings of this kind that a great truth might be established. When human beings come together to seek in inner honesty for the spirit, they also find the way to one another along the paths which lead from soul to soul.

In countless human hearts today the need to find these paths is deeply felt. People say to themselves, 'If anthroposophy is the true view of life, this need of the heart must be felt by those who call themselves anthroposophists.' Yet they must witness how many in the members' groups, advancing anthroposophy as their theoretical conviction, show no sign of this feeling.

Anthroposophical members' meetings must of course make it their task to cultivate the contents of anthroposophy. The knowledge and insight gained by anthroposophy is read and listened to. Anyone who does not see that this must be so is certainly wrong. We should not need an Anthroposophical Society merely for the purpose of debating about all manner of opinions which one may have just as well without anthroposophy. But if we do no more than read anthroposophical writings aloud, or even lecture on anthroposophy as a mere teaching, then it is true that the meetings give us no more than what each of us could gain by reading alone.

Anyone who goes to anthroposophical meetings ought to feel that he is finding *more* there than when he merely studies anthroposophy alone. We should be able to go to the meetings because we find human beings there with whom we like working at anthroposophy. In books about anthroposophy we can find a way of looking at life and the world. In anthroposophical meetings people can find *one another*.

However keenly we read anthroposophical literature, we should be able to feel joy and elation when we go to a gathering of anthroposophists, simply because we are looking forward to meeting the other people there. Then we shall look forward to the meeting even if we expect to hear no more than we have studied long ago and made our own.

An old-established member, finding a new member in his group, should not rest content to feel with satisfaction that anthroposophy has gained another new adherent. He should not merely think, 'Here is another person into whom we can pour anthroposophy,' but he should have a feeling for the fresh human element which comes into the group with the new member.

The essence of anthroposophy is in the *truths* it can help to reveal; the essence of the Anthroposophical Society is in the *life* cultivated there.

It would be the worst possible thing if there were a justification for thinking, 'Valuable as anthroposophy may be, if I want to make a closer contact with people I prefer to go elsewhere than where fanatical, self-satisfied anthroposophists only want to hurl their abstract thoughts at my head with the implication: If you do not think as I do you are only half human.'

Much is done to give rise to such a judgement through,

for instance, the cold didactic impulse to instruct—an easy snare for some, when once they recognize the truth of anthroposophy. On the other hand there is that 'playing at esotericism', so repellent to a newcomer on entering anthroposophical meetings. He will find people who, with a mysterious air, give him to understand that they know many things which 'cannot yet be told to those who are not ready'. But an atmosphere of superficiality pervades all this. Esotericism can only go hand-in-hand with real earnestness and not the vain satisfaction one can draw from prattling about lofty truths. This is far from implying that a sentimental reticence, behind which we shy away from joy and enthusiasm, should be the life element in anthroposophical communities. But to play at withdrawing from 'profane outer life' to pursue 'true esotericism' is incompatible with the Anthroposophical Society. Real life contains on every hand far more that is esoteric than is ever dreamt of by those who repeat, 'We cannot carry on esoteric life in such surroundings; we need a separate gathering for that'.

Undoubtedly gatherings of this kind are often needed; but there is no playing with them. They must be centres of fruitful influence for real life. Esoteric centres, so-called, which only arise to disappear after a short time for lack of serious purpose, can only bring disruptive forces into the Society. Far too often they are but the outcome of a desire to form cliques, the effect of which is to impoverish and not to increase the anthroposophical life in the Society. If we succeed in counteracting the inner falsehood which characterized so much of the talk about esoteric matters in the past, then true esotericism will be able to find a home in the Anthroposophical Society.

To the Members—IV

10 February 1924

The Relation of the Members to the Society

It is understandable that different points of view exist among the members regarding their own relation to the Anthroposophical Society. A person may enter it with the idea that he will find there what he is seeking out of the innermost needs of his soul. In his search and in the finding of what the Society can give him, such a member will then see the meaning and purpose of his membership. I have already indicated that no objection can properly be made to this point of view.

Because of the very essence of anthroposophy, it cannot be for the Society to bring together a circle of human beings and impose upon them, when they enter it, obligations which they did not recognize before, but are expected to take on simply on account of the Society. If we are to speak of obligations in the proper sense it can only be of those of the Society towards its members. But this obvious fact involves another which is not always understood in the right way, and which in fact is often not even considered.

As soon as a member begins to be *active* in any way on behalf of the Society he takes upon himself a great responsibility, a very solemn sphere of duty. Those who do not intend to be thus active should not be disturbed in the quiet spheres of their work; but if a member wants to be active in the Society he must not on any account disregard the fact that in doing so he will have to make the concerns of the Society his own.

It is natural for one who wishes to be a quiet member to say, for example, 'I cannot concern myself with what opponents of the Society say about it.' But this changes the moment he goes outside the sphere of quiet participation.

Then it becomes his immediate duty to pay attention to the opponents and to defend all that is worthy of defence in anthroposophy and the Anthroposophical Society.

That *this* most necessary fact has not always been observed has done the Society no good. Members have the fullest right to expect that in the first place the Society will give them what it promises to give, yet it would surely seem strange to them to be called upon at once to undertake the same obligations as belong to those who hold out these promises.

If, then, we speak of the duties of members to the Society, we can only be referring to those members who desire to be active. This matter must of course not be confused with duties that arise for a person out of anthroposophy itself. But these will always be of a purely human character, and they will only extend the horizons of human responsibility in a way that results from insight into the spiritual world. When anthroposophy speaks in this way it can never mean obligations that apply only in the Anthroposophical Society but will mean duties arising out of a true conception of human nature.

Once more, then, for the members who are active in it the Anthroposophical Society, by its very nature, involves definite responsibilities, and these—for the same reason—must be taken most seriously. A member, for example, may wish to communicate to others the knowledge and perceptions of anthroposophy. The moment his instruction extends beyond the smallest and quietest circle he enters into these responsibilities. He must then have a clear conception of the spiritual and intellectual position of mankind today. He must be clear in his own mind about the real task of anthroposophy. To the very best of his ability he must keep in close contact with other active members of the Society; and it must be far from him to say, 'I am not interested when anthroposophy and those who represent it are placed in a false light or even slandered by opponents.'

The Executive Council formed at the Christmas Conference understands its task in this sense. It will seek to
realize in the Society what has here been expressed, and it
can do no other than ask every member intending to be
active to make him or herself a helper and co-operator in
these matters.

Only in this way shall the Society be equal to the promise
which it holds out to its whole membership—and thereby
to the world at large.

It is really distressing to have, for example, the following
experience. It sometimes happens that would-be active
members meet in a particular place to discuss the affairs of
the Society. They hold meetings especially for this purpose.
In conversation with individuals who take part in these
meetings it will afterwards emerge that they hold certain
opinions about each other, each other's activities for the
Society, and the like—opinions which are not voiced at all
in the meetings. A member, one will find, has no idea what
those who are often associated with him think of his
anthroposophical work. It is absolutely essential that the
impulse given at the Christmas Conference brings things of
this nature into better ways.

Those members above all who claim and desire to be
active in the Society should endeavour to understand this
impulse.

How often does one hear such members say, 'I really
have the goodwill, but I do not know what is the right way
to do things.' We should not hold an all too comfortable
view on this subject of 'goodwill', but ask ourselves again
and again, have we really explored all the channels which
the Society provides to find the right way to act out of
heartfelt co-operation with other members?

To the Members—V

17 February 1924

Anthroposophical Leading Thoughts

In future you will find in these columns some examples of anthroposophical guidelines or leading thoughts.* These are to be thought of as containing advice on the direction which leading members can give to the lectures and discussions in the various groups. They are intended merely as suggestions the Goetheanum would like to make to the whole Society, and they must not infringe on the independent manner of working of the individual leading members. It would be a good thing if the Society were to develop in the direction of providing the scope for the leading members of the different groups to play their part in complete freedom. This will make the life of the Society both richer and more varied.

But it should be possible for a unity of consciousness to arise in the Society, which will happen if the initiative and ideas that emerge at different places become known everywhere. Therefore, in these columns, we shall sum up in short paragraphs the descriptions and lines of thought I have given in lectures to the Society at the Goetheanum. I imagine that those who lecture or conduct the discussions in the groups will be able to take what is given here as guidelines, and develop it in their own way. This will contribute to the unity and organic wholeness of the work of the Society without there being any question of compulsion.

This procedure will become fruitful for the whole Society

---

* See the volume *Anthroposophical Leading Thoughts: Anthroposophy as a Path of Knowledge. The Michael Mystery*, tr. G. and M. Adams (London, Rudolf Steiner Press, 1973).

if it meets with a corresponding gesture, and the leading members inform the Executive Council at the Goetheanum, too, of the substance and form of their own lectures and initiatives. Only then shall we grow from a chaos of separate groups into a Society with spiritual substance.

The guidelines we are going to bring will be as it were themes. Points of contact with them will be found in innumerable places in the anthroposophical books and lecture cycles, so that the subjects thus opened up can be enlarged upon and the discussions in the groups centred round them.

When new ideas emerge from leading members in the several groups, these too can be brought into connection with the suggestions we shall send out from the Goetheanum. We shall thus provide a framework for the spiritual activity in the Society.

Spiritual activity can of course only thrive if the people doing the work can act out of freedom. This is an indisputable truth, and we must not ignore it. But there is no need to sin against it if within the Society the members work in harmony with one another. If such co-operation were impossible, the attachment of individuals or groups to the Society would always remain a purely external thing. In fact we ought to feel that our belonging together is an *inner* reality.

It cannot be tolerated that the existence of the Anthroposophical Society is merely made use of by this or that individual as an opportunity to say what he personally wishes to say for one reason or another. The Society ought to be the centre for the cultivation of what anthroposophy really is. Anything else can, after all, be pursued outside it. The Society is not there for that.

It has not helped us that in recent years individual members have brought into the Society their own personal wishes simply because they thought that as it grew it would become a suitable sphere of action for them. We could ask why this was not dealt with in the way it deserved to be. Yet if that had happened, we should be hearing on all sides, 'Oh, if only the initiative that arose in this or that quarter had been taken up, how much further we should be today!' Well, many things were followed up which came to a sad end and only set us back.

But now we have had enough. The members who wished to experiment in the Society have had their fling. We have given them a try, and such things need not be endlessly repeated. In the Executive Council at the Goetheanum we have a body which intends to cultivate anthroposophy as such, and the Society should be an association of human beings who have the same object in view, and are ready to enter into a living understanding with the Executive Council in the pursuit of it.

We must not think that our ideal can be attained from one day to the next. We shall need time, and patience too. If we imagined that what is contained in the intentions of the Christmas Conference could be realized in a few weeks, this again would be a mistake.

To the Members—VI

24 February 1924

The Quest for Knowledge and the Will for Self-discipline

In the Anthroposophical Society people draw nearer to one another than they would do in other spheres of life. Their common interest in the spiritual life of the world unlocks their souls. It means a great deal to a person to know what inner experiences another has in the course of his spiritual work. People become communicative when they meet someone they know has a willing ear for the things which stir them in their innermost soul.

Therefore it naturally comes about that members of the

Society observe different things in one another—and in another way—than people generally do. But at the same time this involves a certain danger. We learn to value one another when we meet. We feel the most heartfelt joy when the other person opens his soul. All the best things that can grow out of a close friendship may quickly develop. It is obvious that this relationship may just as rapidly turn into over-enthusiasm. Despite its less desirable aspects this ought not merely to be met with cold, heartless matter-of-factness, nor with priggish superiority. Unbridled enthusiasm which has worked its way through to a harmonious state of mind opens up the spirit far more readily than a neutral stance which remains rigid in the face of even the most important things in life.

Still, it may easily happen that those who quickly form a close friendship, no less quickly draw apart again. If you have got to know another person very well indeed because he has poured his heart out to you, you will soon begin to see his weaknesses too, and then the opposite of enthusiasm may ensue. In the Anthroposophical Society this danger is perpetually lurking in the background, and to counteract it is one of the tasks of the Society. So everyone who wants to be a real member should strive in the innermost depths of his soul for inner tolerance towards his fellows. To *understand* the other person—even when he thinks and does things which one would not like to think and do oneself—this should be the ideal.

This need not be synonymous with a lack of discrimination regarding weaknesses and faults. To understand is different from making oneself blind. To a human being whom we love we may speak of his failings, and this will very often be accepted as the greatest service of friendship. However, if we talk down to him with the attitude of an uncaring judge, he will recoil from our lack of understanding, and console himself with feelings of hatred which begin to stir in him against his critic.

In many respects it would be disastrous for the Anthroposophical Society if intolerance toward other people and failure to understand them—so prevalent in the outer world today—were carried into it. Within the Society such qualities grow in intensity through the very fact that people come closer to one another.

These matters indicate most pointedly that the more vital quest for knowledge in the Anthroposophical Society must be accompanied by the necessary endeavour to ennoble and purify the life of feeling. Intensifying the quest for knowledge deepens the life of the soul and reaches down into those regions where pride, conceit, lack of sympathy and many other qualities are lurking.

A lesser quest for knowledge enters these regions only to a slight extent and leaves them slumbering in the deep places of the soul. But a keen and vital struggle for knowledge stirs them from their slumber; habits which kept them under control lose their power to do so. Spiritual idealism may well awaken qualities of soul which would otherwise have remained undisclosed. The Anthroposophical Society should be there to counteract—by cultivating nobility and purity of feeling—the dangers that are lurking in these quarters. There are indeed, in human nature, instincts which instil the fear of knowledge into human beings for the very reason that these connections are felt to exist. But anyone who would refrain from cultivating the quest for knowledge lest it should stir up the uglier feelings in him, fails to develop the fulness of true humanity. It is humanly unworthy to cripple our insight because we fear weakness of character. To cultivate the quest for knowledge and combine it at the same time with the will to self-discipline—this alone is worthy of humanity.

Anthroposophy enables us to do this. We need only reach the inherent vitality of its thoughts; for by their living quality the thoughts of anthroposophy engender power of will, warmth and sensitivity of feeling. It all depends on the individual whether he merely *thinks* anthroposophy or makes it *living* experience.

And it will depend on the members who come forward actively whether their way of representing anthroposophy is only able to suggest thoughts or to kindle the real sparks of life.

To the Members—VII

2 March 1924

The Work in the Society

In the lectures to the Anthroposophical Society which I am now giving at the Goetheanum I am endeavouring to give expression to the basic matters of the life of the human soul.[6] The underlying point of view for these has been indicated in the first five 'leading thoughts' published in the *News Sheet*. My object has been to meet the primary requirement of an anthroposophical lecture. Listeners should have the feeling that when they look into themselves most deeply they realize that anthroposophy is speaking of the first and foremost concerns of their own soul. If we can thus find the right way of presenting anthroposophy there will arise among the members the feeling that *in the Anthroposophical Society the human being is really understood.*

This is the fundamental impulse in those who become members. They want to find somewhere where people are working at a real understanding of human nature.

When we earnestly endeavour to understand the human being we are indeed already on the way to a recognition of the spiritual being of the world. For we are made aware that, with regard to our own human nature, our knowledge of the natural world affords no information, but only gives rise to questions.

If in presenting anthroposophy we tend to lead the soul away from a love of nature, this only leads to confusion. The true starting point of anthroposophical thoughts cannot lie in the belittling of what nature reveals to us. To despise nature, to turn away from the truth which lights up for us from the phenomena of life and the world, or from the beauty that pervades them, and the tasks they set our human will: this frame of mind can at most produce a caricature of spiritual truth.

Such a caricature will always be tinged with the personal element. Even if it is not composed of dreams, it will be experienced in a dreaming way. In waking life we live with other people, and our aim must be to have mutual understanding on things of *common interest*. What each person says must be of importance to the others, and what one individual achieves through his work must have some value for the others. People who live their lives in common must have the feeling that they share the same world. But if a person wallows in his own dreams he cuts himself off from this common world. The dreams of another—even his closest neighbour—may be utterly different from his. In waking life people have a world in common; when they dream they each have their own.

Anthroposophy should lead us, not from waking life to dreaming, but to a more intense awakening. In everyday life we certainly have community, but the experience is within narrow limits. We are relegated to a part of existence, and only in our hearts do we hold the longing for life's fullness. We feel that the common ground of human experience extends beyond the confines of the everyday. And just as we have to look away from the earth to the sun to see the source of light common to all earthly things, so too we must turn away from the world of the senses to the reality of the spirit to find the true sources of humanity where the soul can experience the fullness of community it needs.

Here it may easily happen that we turn away from life instead of entering it more fully and strongly.

The person who despises nature has fallen victim to this danger. He is driven into that isolation of the soul of which ordinary dreaming is a good example. We shall best develop the sense for human truth—which is at the same time universal truth—if we educate our minds by contact with the kind of truth which shines forth from nature into the human soul. The *truths of nature*, experienced with an open, unprejudiced mind, lead us as a matter of course to the truths of the spirit. If we fill ourselves with the *beauty, greatness* and *majesty* of nature, these become a source of true feeling for the spirit. And when we open our hearts to the silent gesture of nature revealing her eternal innocence beyond all good and evil, our eyes are opened to the spiritual world from whence, into the silent gesture, the living Word rings forth, revealing the contrast between good and evil.

Spirit perception, developed by way of a loving perception of nature, enriches life with the true treasures of the soul; spiritual dreaming, elaborated in contradiction to a real knowledge of nature, can but impoverish the human heart.

If one penetrates anthroposophy in its deepest essence one will feel the point of view here indicated to be the one from which all anthroposophical descriptions should take their start. With this as our point of departure we shall come into living touch with the reality of which every member will say, 'There lies the true reason why I entered the Anthroposophical Society.'

It will not be enough for the members who wish to be active in the Anthroposophical Society to be theoretically convinced of this. Their conviction will spring to life only when they develop a real interest in all that goes on in the

Society. As they learn of what is being thought and done by active individuals in the Society they will receive the warmth they need for their own work in it. We must be very interested in other people to meet them in an anthroposophical way. The study of *What is Happening in the Anthroposophical Society* must form the basis of all our activity in it. Those, above all, who wish to be active members will be in need of this.

To the Members—VIII

9 March 1924

The Work in the Society

Members will have observed that in the public lectures which I have given on behalf of the Anthroposophical Society I have taken every opportunity to refer to what our present age knows on the subject of which I am speaking. I did this because anthroposophy must not present itself as a sectarian belief conceived in an arbitrary way. It must express what it really is, namely, the very view of the world and way of life which our age demands.

It seems quite wrong to me when anthroposophists repudiate altogether what people outside anthroposophy are presenting in the spiritual and intellectual sphere. And if, as sometimes happens, we do this in such a way that an expert will immediately perceive we are insufficiently acquainted with the things we refute, anthroposophy will never be able to achieve anything.

The active members in the various groups must be mindful of this. It does not mean that we must arrange *alongside* our anthroposophical lectures others *in addition*, in which the various branches of modern learning are dealt with in the same way as is done outside the Anthro-posophical Movement. This would not achieve the desired end but only create a split—a very painful one—for the anthroposophical members in our audience between the customary type of modern learning and that which should be the real message of anthroposophy.

It is bad to open up a subject and create the impression from the outset that we are only looking for an opportunity to criticize some particular ideas of the present time. We should first of all always consider most carefully whether these ideas may not contain a sound and significant point of departure. In almost every case we shall find that they do. This does not imply that we must reserve all criticism. But we should only criticize when we have first given an objective and appreciative characterization.

If this were borne in mind, something which has recently caused great difficulties in the Anthroposophical Society might disappear altogether. The increased activity among the scientists in our circles can surely call forth only the deepest satisfaction. And yet many members have come to feel that these scientists do not act 'anthroposophically' enough.

In this connection we must mention the attempts which have been made to evolve an anthroposophical conduct as a way of life in various areas and undertakings. Here again many members have come to feel that the conduct of these things has been anything but anthroposophical.

Certainly the criticism that has been levelled at these efforts is only partly justified. For those who pass judge-ment often fail to see the immense difficulties inherent in any such attempt at the present juncture; nor do they appreciate that to do something properly takes time.

Nonetheless this attitude of many of the members is based on a sound feeling. Our first duty as anthro-posophists is to sharpen our soul's vision so as *to see in its true light* what our civilization is producing. For it is characteristic of our age that it makes an endless number of promising discoveries, yet lacks the proper soil in which to plant them. Undoubtedly, in many cases, the very fact that we adopt a positive rather than a negative attitude to them drives us in the end to pass the harshest judgement on them.

As soon as we forget this positive attitude we shall not escape the temptation to hesitate to speak in a truly anthroposophical way. How often do we hear it said, particularly by the scientists in the Society, 'We shall scare the non-anthroposophists away if we start speaking to them of the etheric or astral body.' But our work remains unfruitful if we merely criticize the non-anthroposophists in their domain and yet confine ourselves to lines of thought which can arise equally well in their domain. It is perfectly possible to speak of the etheric and astral bodies if we say why we are doing so.

If we endeavour, however, to speak of all things bearing on anthroposophy in such a way that the anthroposophical quickening of our perceptions is everywhere in evidence, then among the members of the Anthroposophical Society the feeling will disappear that our scientists speak in a manner that is not anthroposophical enough, and that our experts behave in ways that ought not to be expected of members of this Society.

We shall have to set our minds and hearts in this direction if our Christmas Foundation Meeting is not to remain a set of pious wishes, but on the contrary its aims are to proceed towards realization.

To the Members—IX

16 March 1924

The Formulation of Anthroposophical Truths

I have written the above thoughts for members in the hope that they will be discussed among anthroposophists everywhere. I think it would be good if the active members of the Society were to take these thoughts as a starting point so that they can go on from there to help all the members to have a common consciousness of the nature and being of the Anthroposophical Society.

It is certainly right that the main focus in our group meetings should be on discussing anthroposophy and its application to life. But surely in many of the meetings a little time—however short—could be spent on discussing the kind of thing I have suggested. If this is done, many a member will be stimulated to become a true representative of the Anthroposophical Society even in the non-anthroposophical outer world.

It will not do to imagine that the essence and the task of the Anthroposophical Society can be conveyed in a few paragraphs of statutes. Through the fact that anthroposophy sends its impulses deep into our thinking, feeling and will it is itself strongly influenced by each person's inner life. Certainly its main substance can be described in general statements, as is done in so many spheres of intellectual and spiritual life. But necessary as this may be we must not stop short at this. Our general statements will be made alive and richly coloured when each one who carries them in his heart and mind speaks about them out of his own life experience. Indeed, every such individual expression will contribute something of value towards an understanding of the truths of anthroposophy.

If we attach the right importance to this fact we shall

make a discovery: we shall find ourselves continually becoming aware of fresh aspects revealing the real nature of the Anthroposophical Society.

Every active member in the Society will often enough find himself in the position of being questioned about one thing or another. The enquirer is hoping he will learn something from the answers he is given, and the person being asked can also endeavour to learn something from the way the questions are put to him. We should not be inattentive to *this* kind of learning. For these questions will really teach us something about life. Often the particular reason for the question will come to light, and we should be grateful when enquirers can speak to us in this way. They will help us answer questions better and better. What will improve most of all will be the level of feeling that sounds through the words. The feeling content of what we say is an essential part in communicating anthroposophical truths. It is certainly not only a matter of *what* we say, but above all of *how* we say it.

After all, from a certain point of view anthroposophical truths are the most important things that people can communicate to one another. To impart such things to another person without a deep inner feeling of what one is imparting is in fact already to distort them. But this inner feeling is deepened when we perceive in people, however dissimilar they are, the real life background out of which they ask their questions. We do not need to make ourselves into examiners or psychological vivisectors of one another, we can rest content with what the enquirer of his own accord puts into his questions. But no active member of the Anthroposophical Society should ever find satisfaction in answering every question with a hard and fast ready-made pattern. It is often emphasized, and rightly, that anthroposophy must *come to life* in human beings and not remain mere teaching. But a thing can only come to life when it is constantly stimulated by life itself.

If we work in this way in anthroposophy, it will become a stimulus to human love; and indeed in the anthroposophical sphere all our work should be steeped in love. Anyone who has kept his eyes open in the Anthroposophical Society will know that many people come into it because, when the truths of life are presented to them in other quarters, they lack the fundamental quality of human love. The human soul has a delicate sensitivity for perceiving this quality, and it is this, in the highest degree, which forms a medium of understanding.

It may well be asked, 'How can we bring love into a description of earth evolution?' Once we have come to realize that the evolution of the earth and of the universe is only the other side of the evolution of humankind we shall no longer doubt that precisely where these truths are concerned love is the very soul of them.

To the Members—X

23 March 1924

Presenting Anthroposophical Truths

There will be all the more life in the imparting of anthroposophical truths the more they are presented in all kinds of different ways and from the most varied points of view. For this reason active members in the Society should not be afraid of dealing with the same subject again and again in their group meetings. Only they should always approach it from different angles. We shall be led to this quite naturally if our attitude to the questions of others is as I described in my last letter. This way of doing things will really bring us in touch with the *livingness* of anthroposophical insights. We shall feel that every thought image in which we present it *must of necessity be incomplete.* We sense that what we bear in our souls is infinitely richer than what we can express in thought; and as we become more and more clearly aware of this our *reverence* for the life of the spirit is enhanced. And this reverence must be present whenever anthroposophy is being presented. It must be an essential ingredient. Whenever such reverence is absent there is no force in the discussion.

We should never try in some external way to bring this force into our discussions of anthroposophy. We should let it evolve out of the living feeling we have towards the truths of anthroposophy, realizing that as we grasp them in our souls we approach the reality of the spiritual world. This will give the soul a certain mood. There will be moments when the soul will feel itself totally at one with the thoughts about the spiritual world. It is out of this involvement that reverence will quite naturally arise.

The beginning of any real meditation lies in the development of such a mood. Anyone who is unable to love this mood will in vain apply the rules for attaining knowledge of the spiritual world. For it is in this mood that the spark of the spirit which lies in the depths of the human soul is called into consciousness. A human being thereby unites himself with his own spirituality. And it is in this union alone that he can find the spirit in the world. It is solely the spiritual part of us that can approach the spirit in the world.

If the active members of the Society to whom others come for advice can acquire the impetus arising out of such a mood, there will be an increase in them of the capacity to perceive what the other person really wants. It is often hard for a person to put into clear words what moves him most deeply. Therefore it is all too easy for the one who is being asked the question to miss the point of it, and the one who asked the question will rightly feel that he has not received a proper answer. But if he has the mood of soul that comes from such inner feeling as described above, he will have the power to loosen the tongue of the questioner. The latter will then acquire that real, intimate confidence in the person whose advice he is seeking, which brings real life into the communicating of anthroposophical truths. Something will then enter in, enabling the questioner to take the answers he receives as a starting point from which he can proceed independently in the quest of his spiritual needs. He will perhaps have the feeling that although the answer may not have contained all he was seeking, he will now be in a position to help himself further. An inner feeling of strength will come into his soul in place of the powerless feeling he had before. And this feeling of strength was what he was really looking for.

We should not imagine that we shall find the answers to burning soul problems in mere feelings without engaging thought. But a thought produced in cold isolation from the realm of feeling cannot find its way to human hearts. On the other hand we should not be afraid that our feeling might mar the objective nature of our thoughts. For this would happen only if it had *not* found access, by way of the above-mentioned mood of soul, to our human spirituality.

To the Members—XI

30 March 1924

Teaching Anthroposophy

The stimulus to take up anthroposophy will, in most cases, come to a person from his having experienced that looking out into the world outside himself becomes a source of dissatisfaction, and he therefore feels impelled to turn his thoughts to his own human nature. He has a dim feeling that the riddles which life sets him can be illumined not by looking out upon the restless working of the world but by contemplating the inner human being. Thus the striving for world knowledge is transformed into the striving for self-knowledge.

The members who wish to be active in the Anthroposophical Society will have to bear this in mind. Then, on the one hand, they will learn to perceive their task in the right way, while on the other hand they will recognize the dangers involved.

All too often the search for self-knowledge, if led in the wrong direction, grows into a special form of selfishness. A person may take himself too seriously and thereby lose interest in everything going on outside him. In fact *every* right kind of endeavour can lead one astray if it becomes one-sided.

One can reach no real understanding of the world if one does not seek it through an understanding of the human being. For the age-old truth that the human being is a microcosm—a 'miniature world' in fact—will be proved anew time and again. The human being has all the secrets and the riddles of the universe, the macrocosm, concealed within his own nature.

If we take this in the right sense, then every time we look into our inner being our attention will be directed to the world outside us. Self-knowledge will become the gateway to world knowledge. But if we take it in the wrong sense, our study of ourselves will become an imprisonment, and we shall lose interest in the world.

This must not be brought about by anthroposophy. Otherwise we shall never hear the last of the complaint we often hear from many people on entering the Anthroposophical Society: 'Oh dear! What a selfish attitude these anthroposophists have!'

If a person really wants to have self-knowledge, then it should teach him to see more clearly that all his own attributes are there too in other people. We can sense what they feel if we have experienced the same in ourselves. So long as our own experience is lacking, the other person's experience eludes us: we do not see it properly. Or our feeling may become so riveted by our own experience that there is none left for our neighbour's.

If they will be on their guard against these dangers the active members of the Society will then be able to play a helpful part. They will then prevent self-knowledge from degenerating into self-love; in fact they will come to work in the spirit which leads self-knowledge over into philanthropy. And once a person has an interest in his fellow human beings he will certainly not lack an interest in the world in general.

When friends have asked me for a personal verse for a particular purpose I have often given them the following:

If you would know your own being
Look round you on all sides in the world;
If you would truly see and understand the world
Contemplate the depths of your own soul.

The teaching of anthroposophical knowledge must always be in the spirit of this saying. Then we shall avoid the risk that when we discuss our inner being we shall stir up too much egoistic self-absorption.

It is certainly enough to put newcomers off if the first thing they notice is that anthroposophists are only interested in themselves. One becomes aware that people who have been members of the Anthroposophical Society for a while perpetually complain that they do not have enough time really to go into anthroposophy. We find this most often among those whose life work is within the Anthroposophical Movement itself. Their work easily gets too much for them, imagining that this prevents them from meditating and reading anthroposophical literature, and so on. But the love for anthroposophical knowledge must not disrupt our joyful participation in the necessities of life. If it does so, our involvement with anthroposophy will never have the right kind of warmth, but will degenerate into cold selfishness.

Those members who wish to be active in the Society will have to take *this* insight very much to heart. Then they will be able to fill their work with the kind of spirit that can cope with the dangers that so easily arise.

To the Members—XII

6 April 1924

The Structure of Group Meetings

For some time now there has been considerable debate among the members of the Anthroposophical Society as to whether it should become the rule in group meetings to promote, through reading and discussion, a general knowledge of the existing anthroposophical literature, or whether preference should be given to lectures by active members on any subject they choose.

If we give careful thought to the considerations applying to anthroposophical work, we shall realize at once that neither the one nor the other activity must be cultivated exclusively, but that groups should do both, so far as opportunity allows. The availability of anthroposophical literature for members is what brings people into the Society. Its purpose is to form a basis for all that the Society does. If a knowledge and understanding of this literature is promoted in the group meetings it will form a common link, which we need to have if our Society is to have real content and substance.

Let no one make the objection: Whatever is in print I can read for myself at home; I do not need to have that presented to me in group meetings. The error of this view has already been pointed out in these columns. We should appreciate the point of approaching the spiritual treasures of anthroposophy *together* with those others who are united with us in the Society. This feeling of being together and of receiving spiritual treasures together should not be regarded as meaningless.

It is essential that the active members concern themselves with making the available literature into something that, in course of time, really becomes the spiritual possession of the members.

It will not do that many members who have been in the Society for years hear nothing in the group meetings about things of which a certain amount of knowledge is definitely available.

On the other hand it must be said that the life in the Society would suffer serious harm if as many active members as possible were not to make their own individual contributions. This kind of activity can quite well be combined harmoniously with the other. It has to be borne in mind that anthroposophy can only become what it should become when more and more people contribute to its development. We should not rule it out but rather be glad when active members present to a group meeting what they have worked out by themselves.

It is often said that what some people present is not anthroposophy, and in some cases this is justified. But where would we be if we were to sin against the undeniable truth that in the Anthroposophical Society everything should be allowed to live that is part of the spiritual treasures of mankind. The one thing will need to be presented because it can form a basis for further anthroposophical presentations. Another thing will have to be reported so that it can later on be elucidated in an anthroposophical light. So long as the fundamental anthroposophical character is preserved in the Society's work there is no call to set up narrow-minded limitations against what active individuals may bring.

In making the programmes for the group meetings there should be an attempt not to exclude one thing or another, but to include in a balanced way work on the existing literature and presentations by active individuals.

It is not by uniformity but by variety that we shall achieve the goals of the Anthroposophical Society. We should be heartily glad of the fact that we have in our Society so many members who, out of their own initiative, have something to give. We ought to be able to get used to acknowledging such members. There can be real life in the Society only when achievements are properly recognized. Among the faults in our Society a narrow-minded turning down of an offering should be the least common. We should much rather muster the enthusiasm to find out as much as possible about what the various people in the community of anthroposophists have to say.

To the Members—XIII

18 May 1924

The Pictorial Nature of the Human Being

It is very important that it should be understood through anthroposophy that the ideas a person acquires from observing outer nature are inadequate for considering the human being. The ideas which have taken possession of people's minds during the cultural changes of the last few centuries fail to realize this fact. By means of them people have grown accustomed to thinking in terms of natural laws, and they use these natural laws to explain the phenomena which are perceived by the senses. They then turn their attention to the human organism and think that that too can be explained by bringing the laws of nature to bear upon it.

This is just as though, in considering a picture which an artist has painted, we were to take into account only the substance of the colours, their power of adhering to the canvas, the way in which these colours are applied, and similar things. But such a way of regarding a picture does not reveal what is contained in it. Quite other laws are active in the revelation contained in the picture than those which can be perceived by considering such aspects as these.

It is a question of realizing that in the human being something is also being manifested which cannot be grasped from the standpoint of natural law. Once someone has thoroughly made this conception his own, he will be able to understand the human being as a *picture*. A mineral is not a picture in this sense. It reveals only what is directly evident to the senses.

When regarding a picture we look as it were *through* what the senses perceive to its spiritual content. And it is the same when we observe the human being. If we make a thorough study of the human being in the light of natural law, we do not feel that these laws bring us into contact with the essential human being but only with that through which the real human being is manifested.

We must become mentally aware that when we regard a person only from the point of view of natural law it is as if we stood before a picture and saw only 'blue' and 'red', and were quite unable through an inner activity of soul to relate the blue and red to what reveals itself through these colours. When viewing things from the standpoint of natural law we must perceive minerals in one way and the human being in another. In the case of minerals it is for our intellectual understanding as if we were learning about them through a direct sense of touch; in the case of a human being it is as though we were as far away from his essential being as we would be from a picture that we could make a contact with in no other way than through our sense of touch.

Once we have perceived that man is a *picture* of something, we shall have the right attitude of mind to progress to what manifests in this picture.

The pictorial nature of the human being does not manifest solely and alone in one unequivocal way. A sense organ is in its nature least of all a picture, and mostly a kind of manifestation of itself, like a mineral. It is to human sense organs that natural laws come the closest. We have only to look at the wonderful arrangement of the human eye. Natural laws can *approximately* grasp the way this works. And it is similar with the other organs, though it is often not so clearly evident as with the eye. This is because the formation of the sense organs is up to a certain point self-contained. They are inserted into the organism as formations *complete in themselves*, and as such they convey perceptions of the outer world.

It is different in regard to the rhythmic processes in the organism. They do not display a finished form; here, a constant coming into being and passing away of the organism is taking place. If the sense organs were like the rhythmic system we should perceive the outer world as being in a constant state of becoming.

The sense organs are like a picture hanging on the wall. The rhythmic system is comparable to the scene that unfolds when we watch an artist and his canvas during the moments when a picture arises. The picture is not yet there, but is becoming more visible all the time. Our observation shows us a perpetual process of becoming. A thing that has already come into existence remains in existence for a time. When we study the human rhythmic system the passing out of existence, the decomposing process, follows immediately upon the process of becoming, the upbuilding process. The rhythmic system manifests a picture *in the process of change.*

The activity of perceiving with the soul an object which has already become a finished picture can be called *Imagination*, whereas the activity required to comprehend a growing picture is *Inspiration*.

It is different again when we consider the metabolism and system of movement in the human organism. In this instance it is like confronting a completely bare canvas, unused paint pots and an artist who has not yet begun to paint. If you want to understand the metabolic and limb system you must have the kind of perception that has no more to do with what the senses grasp than the bare canvas, the unused paints and the artist have to do with what appears before you later on as the artist's picture. The activity the soul exercises to experience on a purely spiritual level the part of the human being working in the metabolism and the system of movement is the same as when, on seeing the painter, the empty canvas and the unused paints one were to experience the picture to be painted later. To understand the metabolic and limb system the soul has to exercise the power of *Intuition*.

It is necessary that the active members of the Anthroposophical Society should draw attention in this way to the real essence of the fundamentals of an anthroposophical outlook. For we should become aware not only of all the knowledge that can be acquired through anthroposophy but also of how we actually come to *experience* this body of knowledge.

To the Members—XIV

25 May 1924

Regarding the Mood Group Meetings Should Have

By learning to observe the human being in the way spoken of in our last letter the active presence of soul and spirit within the physical and etheric being will be recognized as a fact. When it has become clear that what the senses perceive of the human being is a *picture,* it will readily be understood that something more is at work within the picture than is contained in the material substance of it. Once we recognize the human being as a picture we shall approach him with quite a different attitude of soul than we would if we considered only his material nature and constitution.

This different attitude of soul has the power to wake us up. If we can experience very vividly for a moment what it feels like to see things in this way we shall become aware of the awakening of soul forces which in ordinary life are slumbering. And a great deal depends on whether a person in the very reception of anthroposophy already perceives that other powers of cognition are slumbering in the human soul than those he was conscious of before coming to anthroposophy.

If you know you are looking at a picture you open your mind to what is not perceptible to the senses, and this is the element which now holds your interest, just as in the life of external perception your interest is held by sense-perceptible things.

If the members of the Anthroposophical Society who give lectures would draw the attention of the group members to such an approach, then the teaching of anthroposophy will be accompanied by a real anthroposophical mood.

It is this mood, arising as a matter of course out of such an approach, which will bring to the group meetings the spiritual vitality that should pervade them. Those present will then feel that anthroposophy does not contain only theoretical communications about spiritual matters but is in itself something vigorous and real which leads to the *experience* of the spirit.

It is for the active members to think out in every positive way how this experience of spiritual life can be attained in anthroposophical work.

For only by this means can those who take up anthroposophy, without themselves being capable of direct spiritual investigations, be helped to overcome the feeling that they are only being told theoretically what others, more advanced, can *experience*. If communications about what is experienced in the spiritual world are given in the appropriate way those who listen are able to share in these experiences.

If in the group meetings there is this spirit of sharing in spiritual experience then everything built up on an unjustifiable feeling of authority will be dispelled. The opponents of anthroposophy continually contend that anthroposophists profess obedience to authority in what is imparted to them. If in the Anthroposophical Society anthroposophy is worked out in the right spirit this contention will lose all meaning. For those who come to our meetings would in that case not get the impression that a thing is so merely because someone has said it, but would realize that consent is not enforced in one's own soul but arises from the experience itself.

For example, when you meet a well-disposed person, you do not appreciate his character merely because someone tells you to, but because your own heart immediately feels influenced by his kindly disposition. So too one can become aware of the truth of anthroposophy in that the *way* in which it is communicated gives an intimation of its real character.

The group leaders will have to see to it that anthroposophy is able to work in this way. The esoteric character of anthroposophical gatherings should not depend on creating the feeling that things are being discussed which are mysterious and secret. Esotericism depends on the above-described deepening in the communication of truths, this deepening to be seen in the light of the impulse the Christmas Foundation Meeting endeavoured to bring into the Anthroposophical Society. The never-ceasing intention of keeping our will alive and watchfully in tune with the Christmas Meeting will enable the blessings of those days to be showered more and more on the anthroposophical movement.

To the Members—XV

1 June 1924

More About the Mood Essential in Group Meetings

The study of anthroposophy ought not to lead to a depreciation of external life. True, in the case of many people, it is the hard blows of fate, or a perception of the contradictions of external life, which lead them to a deepening of feeling and incline them to a spiritual understanding of existence.

But just as our physical nature has need of sleep if, when awake, we are to be fit for life, so too, in order that we may enter the spiritual world in a healthy way, we need to participate in the experiences of the physical world in order to develop inner stability and certainty. For the filling of our inner being with spiritual knowledge means an awakening out of the life of sense reality and out of the impulses with which this reality animates the will.

Those who seek to enrich their inner life by undervaluing outer life should indeed be given what they seek in fullest measure, but at the same time this should arouse in them an appreciation of outer life and the ability to handle it with capability. Those of us who are working actively in the Anthroposophical Society should always bear this in mind.

We should constantly remember that human life on earth, looked at from the standpoint of the whole span of human existence in its passage through births and deaths, has its own significance. During earth life the human spirit is embodied in matter. It is dependent on material existence. In no form of existence in the spiritual worlds does the spirit have a similar opportunity to experience what can be experienced through this dependency on material existence.

Life in the material world is, for human beings, that stage of existence when they can perceive the spiritual outside of its reality, *in a picture*. A being which is unable to experience the spirit also in picture-form cannot come to desire the spirit freely, out of its own inner nature. Those beings also, who do not become embodied in material existence as human beings do, pass through stages of life in which they have to surrender their own being to another element of existence.

In this surrender lies the foundation for the development of the impulse of love. A being who has never known what it is to become alienated from its own self is unable to cultivate that devotion to another which manifests as *love*. And the taking in of things of a spiritual nature can easily make a person hard-hearted if connected in a one-sided way with contempt for the manifestations of the outer world.

True anthroposophy does not seek the spirit because it finds nature devoid of spirit and therefore worthy of contempt, but because it wants to seek the spirit *in nature* and can only find this by anthroposophical means.

If we were to develop this attitude in our group meetings the meetings would give the members the kind of experience which would be in harmony with the total demands life makes on us. The unworldliness that can, like an unhealthy atmosphere, so easily enter our work, will be dispelled.

This, too, is one of the elements which should help to bring about the right mood in the work of the Society. The members will not have spent their time in the group meetings in the best way if there is a gulf between what they hear of anthroposophy and what they experience in outer life. The spirit prevailing in group meetings must become a light which continues to shed its rays when members are immersed in the external demands of life. But if this spirit is absent, then anthroposophy will make its members not more efficient but less efficient for life which, after all, also claims its rights. If this were so, many of the reproaches made by outside people against the Society would be justified, and the Anthroposophical Society, instead of promoting anthroposophy would be doing it harm.

To the members—XVI

6 July 1924

More About the Consequences of the Christmas Conference

One of the results of the Christmas Conference should be that those who take it upon themselves to work actively in the Society should present more and more clearly to the world both what the real nature of anthroposophy is and what it is not. So long as it is still possible that our members discuss whether we ought not to slip anthroposophical truths into the conversation here or there without scaring people off by telling them it is anthroposophy—while this thought persists, a number of things in the Anthroposophical Society will not be put right.

It is most important to strive for clarity in this direction. There is a difference between advancing, in a sectarian spirit, a dogmatic form of anthroposophy one has got lined up, and a straightforward, open, sincere and unembellished stand for the insights about the spiritual world which have been brought to light through anthroposophy so that human beings may be able to acquire a relation to this world worthy of humanity.

It is the task of the Executive Council at the Goetheanum unceasingly to carry on the work for anthroposophy with this understanding; and the essential nature of this task must be fully understood by those members who undertake to work actively in the Society. An effect of the Christmas Conference shall be that to an ever greater extent anthroposophy and the Anthroposophical Society shall become one. This cannot happen as long as members of the Anthroposophical Society continue to sow the seeds of controversy between what is 'orthodox' and what is 'heretical'.

Above all one must know the kind of spiritual attitude anthroposophy enables us to have on this matter. It does not consist of a sum of opinions which *must be held* by 'anthroposophists'. Anthroposophists should never ever say, 'We believe this; we repudiate that.' This sort of thing may arise naturally as the result of our anthroposophical study, but it can never be advocated as a programme. The one and only conclusion can be that anthroposophy is in existence; hard work has put it there; I will help the results of this work to become known in the world. It is as yet far too little realized in anthroposophical circles that there is a vast difference between these two attitudes. Otherwise we would not keep on hearing the absurd statement that the Anthroposophical Society believes such and such. In actual fact such a statement means nothing at all, and it is most important we should realize this.

If, for the sake of acquiring a clearer idea of anthroposophy, a person were to ask around concerning the opinions and attitude of a number of members of the Anthroposophical Society, this would be quite the wrong way to get at the nature of anthroposophy. Yet many would-be active members act in such a manner that this predicament is bound to arise. The only justified opinion is: 'Anthroposophy is in the world, and the Anthroposophical Society provides the opportunity to get to know about it.'

On entering the Society for the first time everyone should feel: I am becoming a member simply to *get to know about* anthroposophy. The attitude of the active members can help this feeling to arise in the right way. Nowadays, however, they often produce quite a different result. People are afraid to join the Society because the attitude of active members gives them the impression they must subscribe heart and soul to certain dogmas. Of course this scares them.

We must have the goodwill gradually to remove this impression. Many of the active members think that if people are accepted into the Society merely so that they can get to know about anthroposophy they will leave again when they have found out what they wanted to know, and we shall never have a cohesive Society.

But this will not happen if the active members have the right understanding of the Anthroposophical Society. It will happen, however, if we try to make membership of the Society dependent upon the acknowledgment of even the smallest of dogmas. In fact any point on a programme is a dogma. If the members of the Society are geared to *get to know about* anthroposophy through the members themselves then whether they remain in the Society or not will depend on something quite different, namely whether they can hope to continue to learn something in the Society.

That again will depend on whether the core of the Society is *alive* or dead, and whether in the length and breadth of the Society the conditions are such that the living core will not wither away if the wish is there that it expand into the Society. That the core is alive is the concern and responsibility of the Executive Council at the Goetheanum. The Executive Council does not administer dogmas. It feels solely that it is responsible for a spiritual treasure, the value of which it is fully aware, and its work is to spread this treasure. It is happy whenever someone comes and says, 'I wish to share in what you are doing.' This creates the living form of the Anthroposophical Society. And this will be kept alive if the general attitude and way of working of the active members is in harmony with the Executive Council at the Goetheanum.

Everything that we are justified in calling 'confidence' within the Society can only flourish on a foundation such as this. If this foundation exists, then it will not happen over and over again that the Anthroposophical Society appears to the world as something quite different from what it actually is.

I know quite well what the opinion of many of the active members will be when they read the above. They will say, 'We cannot understand this; now we really do not know what is wanted.' But this is the worst possible prejudice. They should just read the above words *carefully*, and then they will find them neither vague nor ambiguous. To accept them does require a certain sensitivity, but this ought surely to be there in those who want to be active in the Anthroposophical Society.

To the Members—XVII

13 July 1924

A few Words About Understanding the Spirit and Experiencing Destiny

This week I will introduce something into the communications addressed to members in these columns which may serve to bring a further dimension into the work on the Leading Thoughts.

The understanding of anthroposophical insight can be furthered if we are constantly being brought to reflect on the connection between humanity and the world.

If we turn our attention to the world into which we are born and which we leave when we die, we are surrounded in the first place by an abundance of sense impressions. And we form thoughts about these sense impressions.

In bringing the following to our consciousness, 'I form thoughts about the world which my senses reveal to me,' we have come to the point when we can begin to contemplate ourselves. We can say to ourselves: 'I' live in my thoughts. The world gives me the opportunity to experience *myself* in thought. I find myself in my thoughts when I contemplate the world.

Continuing to reflect in this way, the world disappears from consciousness and the 'I' enters in. We stop having mental images of the world and start experiencing the self.

If, conversely, our attention is directed to the inner life in which the world is mirrored, then those events emerge into consciousness which belong to our life's destiny and in which our human self has moved along from the point of time to which our memory goes back. In following up these events of destiny we experience our own existence.

In bringing this to our consciousness: 'My "self" has experienced destiny,' we have come to the point when we can begin to contemplate the world. We can say to ourselves, 'I was not alone with my destiny; the world played a part in my experience. I *willed* this or that; the world flooded into my will. I find the world in my will when I experience this will in self-contemplation.'

Continuing to enter further into our own self, the self disappears from consciousness and the world enters in. We stop experiencing the self and start becoming aware of the world in feeling.

I send my thoughts out into the world; there I find myself; I immerse myself in my own self, there I find the world. If a person experiences *this* strongly enough, he is confronted with the great riddles of the world and of humanity.

For to have the feeling: I struggle hard to understand the world with my thinking, and what is there is after all only myself—this gives rise to the first great riddle. And to feel that one's own self is formed by destiny, yet to perceive in this process the flooding in of events coming from the world—this brings us to the second riddle.

Experiencing this problem of humanity and the world gives rise to the state of mind in which anthroposophy can make a deep impression on a person.

For anthroposophy shows us that there is a way of experiencing the spirit in which we do not lose the world in thinking. We can remain *alive* in thought. Anthroposophy tells us that meditation is an inner experience in which we do not lose the sense world when we think, but gain access to the spirit world. Instead of penetrating into the ego in which the sense world is felt to disappear, we penetrate into the spirit world where the ego feels strengthened.

Anthroposophy shows further that there is a way of experiencing destiny in which we do not lose the self. In our destiny, too, we can still feel ourselves *to be active*. Anthroposophy points to an impartial, unegoistic observation of human destiny as the kind of experience in which we learn to love the world and not only our own existence. Instead of staring into the world which bears the ego along on its waves of joy and sorrow, we find the ego which shapes its own destiny voluntarily. Instead of striking against the world on which the ego is dashed to pieces we penetrate into the self which feels itself united with the events of the world. Our human destiny comes to us from the world that is revealed to us by our senses. If we find our own activity present in the working of destiny our own self rises up before us not only out of our own inner being but out of the sense world too.

If we are able to feel, however faintly, that the spiritual part of the world appears in the self, and that the self proves to be at work in the outer world of sense, we have already learnt to understand anthroposophy properly.

For we shall develop a sense for realizing that in anthroposophy it is possible to describe the spirit world as being comprehended by the self. And with this sense we shall also realize that in the outer world the self can be found in a different way from immersing ourselves in our inner being. Anthroposophy finds the self by showing that the sense world reveals to us not only sense perceptions but also the after-effects of our life before birth and our former earth lives.

A human being can now look out into the world of the senses and say: there is really not only colour, sound and warmth there; the experiences passed through by souls before their present earthly life are also active there. And he can look into himself and say: not only my ego is there; also a spiritual world comes to manifestation there.

It is in an understanding of this kind that a person who has come to grips with the great riddles of the world and humanity can find common ground with the initiate who, in accordance with his insight, is obliged to speak of the outer world of the senses as manifesting not only sense perceptions but also the impressions of what human souls have done in their life before birth and past earthly lives;

and who has to say of the world of the inner self that it reveals spiritual qualities which give as powerful an impression as do the perceptions of the sense world.

The active members should consciously take it upon themselves to be mediators between the feelings that questioning souls have about the great riddles of the world and humanity and the descriptions initiation knowledge gives us of drawing forth a past world out of the destiny of human beings, and of opening up a perception of a spirit world through a strengthening of the soul.

In this way, through the work of the active members, the Anthroposophical Society can become a true preparatory school for the school of initiates. It was the intention of the Christmas Conference to point to this most forcibly; and the ones who truly understand what this conference meant will continue to point this out until there is sufficient under-standing of it for the Society to be brought fresh tasks.

To the Members—XVIII

10 August 1924

How the Leading Thoughts are to be Used

The Leading Thoughts issued by the Goetheanum are meant to be of help to the active members to bring unity into the anthroposophical work. Following them week by week, they will be found to lead to further study of the material available in lecture cycles and to the bringing of this in a certain order.

It would of course be far better if the lectures given in Dornach were immediately to be sent out each week to all the various groups. But we ought also to realize what complicated technical arrangements would be required to do this. The Executive Council at the Goetheanum will certainly endeavour to do everything possible to bring this about. But we must reckon with the available possibilities. The intentions that were expressed at the Christmas Conference will certainly be realized. But it takes time.

At present it is an advantage to a group if it has members who visit the Goetheanum and hear lectures and can give a report of them at their meetings. And the groups should realize the benefit of sending members to the Goetheanum to perform this function. Yet the work already achieved in the Anthroposophical Society, and that which is available in the printed cycles and lectures,[7] must not be unduly undervalued. If you take out these lecture cycles and call to mind from the title what is contained in the one or the other, and then turn to the Leading Thoughts, you will find that you discover one thing in one cycle and another in another which further elaborates the Leading Thoughts. By bringing passages together that are scattered over the various cycles you will find the various aspects with which to expand the Leading Thoughts.

We are behaving in the Anthroposophical Society in a really wasteful manner if we make no use at all of the printed cycles, but always want only the latest from the Goetheanum. It will also be readily understood that in course of time there would no longer be any possibility of printing the cycles if they were not made full use of.

There is still another aspect to consider. In spreading the contents of anthroposophy it is absolutely essential to be conscientious and responsible. The things said about the spiritual world must be brought into a form in which there is no risk of the pictures of the spiritual facts and beings being misunderstood. Anyone who hears lectures at the Goetheanum will receive an immediate impression. If he reproduces the contents, this impression will still echo in him, and he will be capable of formulating them so that they can be understood properly. But if they are repeated at second or third hand the probability of inaccuracies creeping in becomes greater and greater. All these things should be borne in mind.

And a further aspect is probably the most important of all. The point is not that anthroposophy should be listened to or read only superficially, but that it should be taken up by the life in one's inner being. It is essential that it lives on both in one's thinking and in one's feeling; and the Leading Thoughts are really intended to encourage this with regard to the published lecture cycles. If this aspect is not sufficiently considered, then the Anthroposophical Society will continue to fall short of presenting the real being of anthroposophy. People deceive themselves if they say: What use is it to me to hear all these things about the spiritual worlds if I cannot see those worlds myself? What they do not realize is that it will help them acquire this vision if their attitude to anthroposophical work is in accordance with what was indicated above. The lectures at the Goetheanum are presented in such a way that their content can live on and work freely in the minds and hearts of the hearers. The same applies to the contents of the lecture cycles. They do not contain dead material to be imparted superficially, but the sort of subject matter which, when viewed from various aspects, will stimulate a vision for seeing spiritual worlds. It should not be thought that on the one hand you listen to the contents of the lectures and on the other hand you get to know the spiritual world separately by means of meditation. In this way you will never make real progress. Both activities must work together on the soul. And to work further with anthroposophical ideas both with your thinking and your feeling is also exercising the soul. You will begin to develop *spiritual vision* if you proceed with anthroposophy in the way described.

In the Anthroposophical Society far too little importance is attached to the fact that anthroposophy should not be a lifeless theory but life itself. Life is its very nature, and if it is *made into* a dead theory then often enough it is not a *better* theory at all but one that is worse than the others. But it becomes a theory only when it is *made into* one, by killing it. It is still not sufficiently realized that anthroposophy is not only different from other world conceptions but that it *has to be received in a different way*. Its nature is recognized and experienced only when people receive it in this different way.

The Goetheanum should be looked upon as the essential centre of anthroposophical work and activity, but one ought not to lose sight of the fact that the anthroposophical material which has been worked out should also be given its due in groups. The activities taking place at the Goetheanum can in a living sense gradually become the possession of the whole Anthroposophical Society when as many members as possible come to the Goetheanum itself bringing with them the life of their own groups and participating to their utmost in the active work going on at the Goetheanum. All this, of course, has to be worked out with real enthusiasm and warmth of heart; for that quality will be lacking in a superficial report of the work each week. The Executive Council at the Goetheanum will need time and sympathetic understanding on the part of the members. Then it will surely be able to work in the spirit of the Christmas Conference.

Notes and References to Part Two

After the 'Christmas Conference 1923–24' Rudolf Steiner wrote 'Letters to the Members' every week until his death on 30 March 1925 in the new organ of the Society *Was in der Anthroposophischen Gesellschaft Vorgeht* (What is happening in the Anthroposophical Society), and from the fifth letter onward these letters were accompanied by Leading Thoughts. These Leading Thoughts with their accompanying essays are to be found in *Anthroposophical Leading Thoughts*, Rudolf Steiner Press, London 1973. However, all those essays dealing exclusively with the creating of a new form for the Society and essays about the School for Spiritual Science, all the existing communications and announcements, and the lectures, meetings and addresses referring to them, have been put together in the volume *Die Konstitution der Allgemeinen Anthroposophischen Gesellschaft und der Freien Hochschule für Geisteswissenschaft 1924/25* (GA No. 260a). The 'Letters to the Members' presented here are a separate edition out of the above-mentioned volume. Marie Steiner first published them in book form in 1930 and they were also contained in *An die Mitglieder* (Achtzehn Briefe). *Das Michael-Mysterium*, Dornach 1930; in *Anthroposphische Leitsätze*, Dornach 1954.)

1. See Rudolf Steiner, *The Christmas Conference for the Foundation of the General Anthroposophical Society 1923/24* (Anthroposophic Press, 1990).
2. See Rudolf Steiner, 'The Laying of the Foundation Stone of the General Anthroposophical Society' contained in the volume *The Christmas Conference*, op. cit.
3. The double-domed building of the First Goetheanum, built entirely of wood, was destroyed by fire on New Year's Eve, 1922.
4. See Rudolf Steiner, 'Das Goetheanum in seinen zehn Jahren', contained in the volume *Der Goetheanumgedanke inmitten der Kulturkrisis der Gegenwart* (The conception of the Goetheanum in the midst of the cultural crisis of the present). Collected essays from *Das Goetheanum* 1921–1925 (GA No 36).

5. While discussing this paragraph during the Christmas Conference Rudolf Steiner wanted to include the following sentence:

'A specified number of members, the number to be determined from time to time according to the regulations, may ask for an extraordinary general meeting at any time.'

This sentence was missing the first time the Statutes appeared, in the *News Letter* of 13 January 1924. However, according to article 64 of Swiss civil law, the law permits a fifth of the membership of any society to call an E.G.M.

6. See Rudolf Steiner, *Karmic Relationships*, a series in eight volumes (Rudolf Steiner Press, London). The volumes I–IV contain the 51 lectures given in Dornach in 1924, the volumes V–VIII are lectures given on this theme in other places.

7. Numerous lecture cycles and single lectures by Rudolf Steiner were published by Marie Steiner in the Philosophisch-Anthroposophischer Verlag (formerly Philosophisch-Theosophischer Verlag). They are now in the section of the *Gesamtausgabe* (Complete Works) under the heading 'Lectures to Members of the Anthroposophical Society'.